Lee Harwood

Also by Lee Harwood:

Poetry
title illegible
The Man with Blue Eyes
The White Room
Landscapes
The Sinking Colony
Freighters
H.M.S. Little Fox
Boston–Brighton
Old Bosham Bird Watch
Wish you were here (with Antony Lopez)
All the Wrong Notes
Faded Ribbons
Monster Masks
Crossing the Frozen River : selected poems
Rope Boy to the Rescue
In the Mists: mountain poems
Morning Light
Evening Star
Collected Poems
Gifts Received

Prose
Captain Harwood's Log of Stern Statements and Stout Sayings.
Wine Tales: Un Roman Devin (with Richard Caddel)
Dream Quilt : 30 assorted stories
Assorted Stories : prose works
Not the Full Story: 6 Interviews (with Kelvin Corcoran)

Translations
Tristan Tzara *Cosmic Realities Vanilla Tobacco Dawnings.*
Tristan Tzara *Destroyed Days, a selection of poems 1943-1955.*
Tristan Tzara *Selected Poems*
Tristan Tzara *Chanson Dada: selected poems*
Tristan Tzara *The Glowing Forgotten : A Selection of Poems.*

LEE HARWOOD

Selected Poems

Shearsman Books
Exeter

Published in the United Kingdom in 2008 by
Shearsman Books Ltd
58 Velwell Road
Exeter EX4 4LD

www.shearsman.com

ISBN 978-1-905700-93-6

Acknowledgements
All of the poems reprinted in this volume have been taken from Lee Harwood's
Collected Poems (Shearsman Books, Exeter, 2004), with the exception of those in the
final section. 'Cloudy Sunday' and 'Comparative anatomy' first appeared in *Shearsman*
n° 75/76; 'Frames' was first printed in *Zoland Poetry*; the poems from 'Gifts Received'
first appeared in a limited edition collection of the same name from Artery Editions,
Hove.

CONTENTS

FOREWORD

These *Selected Poems* range from 1965 to 2007. The titles given to the sections in the contents list generally correspond to the books where the poems first appeared, though not always. Some recent uncollected poems are also included.

Over these years I think, and hope, I've changed in the way I see the world. It would seem natural that there should be a parallel development in my writing. Re-reading these poems, however, I realise there are often repetitions and echoes, insistences that remain throughout on or under the surface. A reader will soon recognise them, despite shifts in the scenery.

The poems, I imagine, harbour curious stories, questions and explorations, instructions for assembling pictures, declarations of love and other obsessions, elegies, and often enough a collage of all these things. They set off, one hopes, into the unknown or barely guessed at. It's in the reader's hands.

Language is never perfectly reliable but—obvious enough—it's all we have to talk to one another. It's to be used as well as possible, as precisely and clearly as possible, but not to be wholly trusted. The complexity of language and people and "life" is to be worked with, accepted, and all their contradictions to be relished. I learnt this, and ways of mapping it all, early on when still in my teens from reading Ezra Pound, and then a year or two later from Tristan Tzara, Jorge Luis Borges, and John Ashbery. After that the list of writers I'm indebted to spreads far and wide, whether it be the thought and imagination of Jack Spicer or the sharpness and heart of Anne Stevenson or the amused tenderness of Constantine Cavafy. My thanks to them all.

I would also like to thank the editors and publishers who over the years have brought out my books. My thanks too to the editors of the magazines where these poems first appeared. Their work and care is a generous encouragement for any writer. And finally a whole heap of thanks to Kelvin Corcoran, John Hall and Robert Sheppard for helping make this selection. Their advice made this, I hope, a more varied and balanced choice of poems than I could ever have done on my own.

Lee Harwood

AS YOUR EYES ARE BLUE

As your eyes are blue
you move me—and the thought of you—
I imitate you.
and cities apart. yet a roof grey with slates
or lead. the difference is little
and even you could say as much
through a foxtail of pain   even you

when the river beneath your window
was as much as I dream of. loose change and
your shirt on the top of a chest-of-drawers
a mirror facing the ceiling and the light in a cupboard
left to burn all day   a dull yellow
probing the shadowy room   "what was it?"

"cancel the tickets"—a sleep talk
whose horrors razor a truth that can
walk with equal calm through palace rooms
chandeliers tinkling in the silence as winds batter the gardens
outside   formal lakes shuddering at the sight
of two lone walkers
                              of course this exaggerates
small groups of tourists appear and disappear
in an irregular rhythm of flowerbeds

you know even in the stillness of my kiss
that doors are opening in another apartment
on the other side of town   a shepherd grazing
his sheep through a village we know
high in the mountains the ski slopes thick with summer flowers
and the water-meadows below with narcissi
the back of your hand and—

a newly designed red bus drives quietly down Gower Street
a brilliant red   "how could I tell you . . ."
with such confusion
                              meetings disintegrating

and a general lack of purpose only too obvious
in the affairs of state
                    "yes, it was on a hot july day
with taxis gunning their motors on the throughway
a listless silence in the backrooms of paris bookshops
why bother   one thing equal to another

dinner parties whose grandeur stops all conversation

but
      the afternoon sunlight which shone in
your eyes as you lay beside me watching for . . .—
we can neither remember—still shines as you
wait nervously by the window for the ordered taxi
to arrive   if only I could touch your naked shoulder
now   "but then . . ."

and the radio still playing the same
records I heard earlier today
                        —and still you move me
and the distance is nothing
"even you—

THE WHITE AND BLUE LINER LEFT HARBOUR AND BEGAN TO CROSS THE OCEAN AGAIN

the lone hunger of wolves on ice blue days
a sleigh with tugging yapping dogs passed through the forest
and I was still nowhere near you
autumn was the same in seaside towns
as it was in the dark mill-town valleys of the north
the rain beating down on the sodden hill-side
to tell you of the warmth indoors seems
too irrelevant—
                    a kiss gone forever
is too easy to understand that I have to stay
silent
the leap back into cafes and juke-boxes
again is too simple a reaction that I
follow it and am surprised that it works

"the deserted houses and empty windows
what can I say"

just fold it up and pack away
a tangle of circumstances

Summer

these hot afternoons "it's quite absurd" she whispered
sunlight stirring her cotton dress inside the darkness when
an afternoon room crashed not breaking a bone or flower.
a list of cities crumbled under riots and distant gun-fire
yet the stone buildings sparkle. It is not only
the artificial lakes in the parks . . . perhaps . . .
but various illusions of belonging fall with equal noise and regularity
how could they know, the office girls as well
"fancy falling for him . . ." and inherit a sickness
such legs fat and voluptuous . . . smiling to himself
the length of train journeys

the whole landscape of suburban railway tracks,
passive canals and coloured oil-refineries.
it could be worse—

at intervals messages got through
the senate was deserted all that summer
black unmarked airplanes would suddenly appear
and then leave the sky surprised at its quiet
"couldn't you bear my tongue in your mouth?"

skin so smooth in the golden half-light
I work through nervousness to a poor but
convincing appearance of bravery and independence

mexico crossed by railways. aztec ruins
finally demolished and used for spanning one more ravine
in a chain of mountain tunnels and viaducts
and not one tear to span her grief
to lick him in the final mad-house hysteria
of armour falling off, rivets flying in all directions like fire-crackers,
and the limp joy of the great break-down
which answers so many questions.
a series of lovers—but could you?—
all leading through the same door after the first hours
of confused ecstasies.

the dream woman who eats her lover.
would suffocation be an exaggeration of what really happens?
the man who forgets, leaving the shop
without his parcels, but meaning no harm.
"it's all a question of possession,
jealousy and . . ." the ability to torment,
the subtle bullying of night long talkings.
what artificial fruits can compare with this
and the wrecked potting-sheds that lie open
throughout the land? gorging their misery
and that of others . . . geranium flowers hacked off the plants
by gentlemen's canes and now limp on the gravel
    paths wandering through empty lawns and shrubberies
afternoon bickerings on a quiet park bench while
families take tea at a convenient cafe, so nicely situated.

engines and greased axles clattering through the shunting-yards.
fluttering parasols running for cover
under the nearby elms as the first heavy sweet raindrops
lick the girls forehead. the slightly hysterical
conversations crowded beneath the leaking branches
waiting for the july thunder to pass. The damp heat
and discomfort of clothes, a tongue passing the length
of her clitoris . . . and back again . . .
erections in the musty pavilion which should lead to a lake
but doesn't. the resin scent and dry throat in the pine wood
across the meadows.
              "surely you remember?"
but so long ago.

strawberries lining her lake in the dark woods
an old picture slowly fading on the wall
as if a flower too could change her face
as a dusk cloaks our loneliness

LANDSCAPE WITH 3 PEOPLE

1

When the three horsemen rode in
you left me
there was no great pain at your leaving
if I am quite honest
you disappeared back into the house
and I mounted up and rode out with the men

It is strange that now many years later
aboard this whaler I should remember
your pink dress and the crash of the screen door

2

The roses tumbled down through the blue sky
and it was time for us to go out
Our horses were saddled and the peon waited patiently
The morning was still cool and quiet—a low
mist was still staring at our horses' hooves.
So we rode round the estate till 10 o'clock
—all was well.

Later at my desk—the accounts settled—I would
take a thin book of poems and read
till he brought me my dry martini
heavy ice cubes clattering in the tumbler
and vodka like sky-trailers gradually
accepting the vermouth and sky.
but this was a different ranch

and my dreams were too strong to forget
a previous summer. And what did it matter
that the excitement and boredom were both states
to be escaped except a grey   lost   and on
these mornings a ship would sink below the horizon
and winter covered the islands   a deserted beach

3

Once it was simpler, but in those
days people rarely left the city
It was quite enough to stand on the
        shingle bank when the tide was out
and the sun was setting and workmen
would lean forward to switch on television sets.

4

on winter evenings I would come across her by accident
standing in bookshops—
she would be staring into space dreaming
of—that I never knew

And most of this is far from true—
you know—we know so little
even on this trite level—but he—he was
more beautiful than any river

and I am cruel to myself because
of this and the indulgence it involves.

I loved him and I loved her
and no understanding was offered
to the first citizen
when the ricks were burnt.

THE ARGENTINE

1

Of course I was discontent with the ranch
the pampas was only there for one purpose
that the whole land knew of

The green continent groaned and stretched
while its brown rivers charged round in all directions
only to settle down as before
when the land fell asleep again

A single tree dominated the mountain top
but went no further than that

So many wrong and arrogant statements were
made in the geography books—and I
was not alone in resenting these

Brown chaos charged the towns and finally
smashed through into the very heart
of the people—they were terrified and some of
the people died too

"Can't you understand my difficulties?" was
whispered as I put my ear to the ground
"I wasn't prepared, and she could not wait
for ever"   the voice went on and on
with an endless story

I kicked every door down in the house
but found no one
It was opportune that at this moment
the group of horsemen galloped into
the court-yard. I had seen them at this
same time last year—but this time
I was prepared to ride away with them.

2

This was not the first migration
nor would this country be in anyway final—
the movement had been an agony dragged across
many lands   it was a well known process

The dead and numbed tundra or the sleepy estuary
with its brown banks and heavy jungle
"The grass was always greener on the other side"

She understood, I thought, that the ritual was grotesque
as it was necessary—and all this belonged elsewhere
just as the real love was elsewhere, but
this through accident and not desire

3

"He never visited the ranch"—and so in isolation
I continued as best I could. No profits were made
but neither were there any losses to talk of
What made it bearable was the memory—and hope—
an airport lounge with its automatic clock
and the milling crowds at the bus terminal . . .
He had a way of looking across a dinner table
—it at once commanded and yet asked for kindness.
Love and tenderness were the dominants—and the ceremony
of social acts was all that separated a fulfilment.
In fact pleasure was gained by the very anticipation,
by the polite dinner conversations and the easy talk
in the bars afterwards
The brief touch of his hand
or the caress of legs under a table
gave more than any previous experience

When these memories grew unbearable . . .
The mountains   the long ride and brief visits to other ranches
where nervousness made an evening pass quickly enough
in a series of laborious politenesses

On the way home, rain beating on the car roof
the essential notation of details like
the car's head-lamps and the night—their effect on one another
All this seized in weak desperation to distract
a realisation, and sometimes even a regret

Such an image had been set so deep in my heart
that its destruction would inevitably cause
much more than local damage
and the fire chief didn't exaggerate when he said
"keep all those people well clear. That building's
going to collapse any minute.
It's little more than a burnt-out shell"

4

How could the two see reality as far as it meant
the truth of their situation or rather how true
were their words and sensations—both come and go
quite rapidly after all.

On the sidewalk in Fifth Avenue just below 12th Street
3 men were parting outside a German restaurant.
The older one had to go uptown—it was late—
and the 2 young men were
separately going to drift round the Village for a few hours
Then, as the taxi arrived, Joe reached up
and kissed John on the forehead.
The 3 split up. It was a hot june night—of course.

The second young man left outside this action
evidently felt something
It would seem that he was really the more concerned
with the older man and that he now regretted
his passiveness in that street, but he had had a reason
—though now it seemed a mistaken one.
He had feared to embarrass, where in fact a spontaneous act . . .

The frustration at a missed chance is universal
and a slight jealousy of the successful equally common

There were other days, and usually the older and the younger man
succeeded in gaining some degree of harmony

But . . .
the pressure of a train and a plane schedule
put a simple end to that development

Finding a torn letter left in a hotel room
he read—"she must have felt something for me,
but I was torn in two,
and in the end I just waited for her to come to me
—and this got me nowhere, as she too had her fears
and I was not the only answer in that town."

5

Mist rose from the marshes
and the rider was forced to skirt the estuary
and keep to the higher ground. Dew was heavy on
the coarse grass. The grazing lands stretched as far
as the eye could see in all directions.
And above this vast open countryside rose a hot sun
that soon thrust the mist back into the ground.

The cocks crowed and the horses grew restless
for the coming day's work. The dogs barked
and strained at their leashes as the first men
fed and watered the horses. This was the beginning . . .
Then midday.   Evening time   the faint sound of voices
from the other side of the yard

6

The rare view from the mountain pass
suddenly made everything seem clear
and the whole geography somehow too simple
The answers were obvious and the route through
all the country ahead

The journey had to be made and the horsemen were right
But the weight of possessions held on to,
if not for love of them, then for some sense of duty
and fear

These accounts of past and future journeys
became boring . . . and any violence that might have been
has now grown limp like the vase of dead flowers
that the efficient house-keeper will surely clear away

THE TRACTORS ARE WAITING

in the pain of silence
the meadows . . .
and from the barn's top loft
but nothing rustled among the bales of straw
the tractor is waiting in the meadow
but flowers arranged in a vase are no real comfort
     despite their scent

if an obsession were carried to its limit
then there would be a clean sky across
which grey clouds lovingly—and a lone
farmhouse stands out on the flat horizon
its plank walls bleached and the wheat
coarse and hard

THE DOOMED FLEET

1

The entire palace was deserted, just as was
the city, and all the villages along the 50 mile
route from the seaport to the capital.
It was not caused by famine or war—
"It was all my fault."

The troops of desperate cavalry were ridiculous.
The naval guns could pick off
whatsoever their whim dictated,
but there was only one commander-in-chief.

2

The grey battleships lay in silence
anchored in the middle of the harbour.
They were ready all the time—
the only necessity in all this was decisions.
That may appear laughable—it's all
so simple.

The wounded was a subject never touched on
in the officers' mess. And the question of
occasional small but brutal outbreaks of
disease was similarly treated.

Nothing that could disturb the carefully planned
vanity was tolerated. That was the new order.

3

Grey waves slapped against the sides of
the iron grey battleships. Seabirds screeched
above the wind; they don't sing.

Even the ships appeared deserted, except
for the occasional dark figures that would
hurry along a deck and then disappear
through a hatch-way as abruptly as when they first
appeared. It was their continual menace,
however, that undeniably asserted their presence.

The menace. The power that vibrated
from the ships. The grey harbour.
Power. Menace. All terminals irrelevant.

In such a setting, it is not surprising
that tears or tenderness, shown by a small
but delicate gesture or caress, were of no consequence.

The men's minds were set—
they didn't understand "pity". The very word
had been deliberately deleted from all the books
scattered among the fleet. They needn't have feared.

4

With so few exits left . . .
"That was really ridiculous, wasn't it?"
Murder was just one of the expected events.
It would be carried out with the precision
of any naval operation and with the coldness.
Everyone knew their place and to disrupt the
series would be not so much reprehensible
as an admission of bad breeding in the extreme.

It was only actual closeness to the event
that allowed any levity. The midshipmen were
only boys, after all. And the officers and the men . . . ?
—who is ever free from the fears and shadows
so firmly established in every childhood?
The point of "safe return" had long since been passed.
There were no maps in existence
for this ocean, nor were there any charts

of seas, harbours or sheltered estuaries
where the least clue or news-item
might be found concerning "The Successful Voyage".

Maybe they never did get there and, instead,
the whole expedition lay at the bottom.
This already begins to sound like a very bad boy's story.

5

Age began to show . . . and the divisions widen
and become even more resolute and rigid.
"What could have been" became altogether another story
like the family photos in the captain's wallet
—there was no room for sentimentality now.

The heavy service revolver seemed somehow too
melodramatic to be real enough for its purpose.
I suppose there was no doubt about efficiency
—only about motives. Wasn't this word
"melodramatic" something of a key?
How *real* was the death to be?
Was it an act of necessity or escape, or
one last weak self-justification, self-gratification . . . ?
The scene was, apart from superficial changes,
only too familiar, and tired.
The unwilling audience would at least be glad
of the concrete finality of this latest show.
It couldn't have much of a sequel, thank God.

The chart table was cluttered with empty coffee cups
and a haze of cigarette smoke filled the navigator's cabin.
It was very late at night, and the navigator
had fallen asleep, fully clothed and exhausted.
But even now, with so much unanswered and so much confusion,
there was in the atmosphere a feeling of finality
whose very grimness brought a strange joy
and relief. The death would not be that dark—

The dead body somehow would know a sweetness
that can be compared to the parable of the
bees' honey inside the dead lion's carcass.

The fleet steamed out beyond the point.
Nothing was free from the ridiculous and "pain."
The laughter was not disrespectful,
nor was it really that inappropriate.
The night sky was a dark blue and most stars visible.
Salt waves broke over the rusted iron decks.

WHEN THE GEOGRAPHY WAS FIXED

for Marian

The distant hills are seen from the windows.
It is a quiet room, and the house is in a town
far from the capital.
The south-west province even now in spring
is warmer than the summer of the north.
The hills are set in their distance
from the town and that is where they'll stay.
At this time the colours are hard to name
since a whiteness infiltrates everything.
It could be dusk.
The memory and sound of chantings
is not so far away—it is only a matter
of the degree of veneer at that moment.
This is not always obvious and for many
undiscovered while their rhythm remains static.
It's all quite simple,
once past the door—and that's only a figure
of speech that's as clumsy as most symbols.
This formality is just a cover.

The hills and the room are both in
the white. The colours are here
inside us, I suppose. There's still a tower
on the skyline and it's getting more obscure.
When I say "I love you"—that means
something. And what's in the past
I don't know anymore—it was all ice-skating.
In the water a thick red cloud
unfurls upwards; at times it's almost orange.
A thin thread links something and there are
fingers and objects of superstition
seriously involved in this.

The canvas is so bare
that it hardly exists—though the painting

is quite ready for the gallery opening.
The clear droplets of water sparkle
and the orange-red cloud hangs quite seductively.

There is only one woman in the gallery now
who knows what's really happening on the canvas—
but she knew that already, and she
also instinctively avoided all explanations.
She liked the picture and somehow the delicate
hues of her complexion were reflected in it.
She was very beautiful and it soon became
obvious to everyone that the whole show
was only put on to praise her beauty.
Each painting would catch one of the colours
to be found in her skin and then play with it.
Though some critics found this delicacy
too precious a conceit, the landscape
was undeniable in its firmness
and the power that vibrated from the
colours chosen and used so carefully.

During the whole gallery-opening a record of primitive red
indian chants was played—and this music
seemed to come from the very distant hills
seen in every painting—their distance was
no longer fixed and they came nearer.
But recognitions only came when all
the veneer was stripped off
and the inexplicable accepted in the whiteness.

QUESTION OF GEOGRAPHY

Facing the house   the line of hills
across the valley   a river somewhere
hidden from view   the thickets there
I can't remember   the colours
green   a rich brown   as the sun shone
turned to slate grey   at times a soft blue smudge
with dusk or rain clouds   the details obscured
but like a long ridge setting the skyline
Months gone by   the seasons now almost full circle

It was spring and our garden was thick with
primroses
Each morning I would go out and . . .

Ridge in the distance   everything the same
as before   it must be
The moors edged with pine woods
in the south–west province   a repetition
but the cathedral town unchanged
It makes no difference who was there
all inevitably reduced to the question of
geography or memory

And now awaiting the next spring
set in yet another place   this too with
its own colours and forms
the others seeming somehow irrelevant in the present excitement
but still real like a very sure background
—you paint over the picture and start on
the new one   but all the same it's still there
beneath the fresh plains of colour

THE "UTOPIA"

The table was filled with many objects

The wild tribesmen in the hills,
whose very robes were decorated with designs
of a strangeness and upsetting beauty
that went much further than the richly coloured silks
embroidered there could ever suggest; . . .

There were piles of books, yet each one
was of a different size and binding.
The leathers were so finely dyed. The blues
and purples, contrasting with the deceptive simplicity
of the "natural" tans.
And this prism and arrangement of colours
cannot be set down—the fresh arrangements
and angles possible can only point through a door
to the word "infinite" made of white puffy clouds
floating high in a blue summer sky;
this has been written there by a small airplane
that is now returning to its green landing field.

The table is very old and made of fine mahogany
polished by generations of servants.
And through the windows the summer blue skies
and white clouds spelling a puffy word.
And on the table the books and examples
of embroidery of the wild hill tribesmen
and many large and small objects—all of which
could not help but rouse a curiosity.

There are at times people in this room
—some go to the table—things are moved—
but the atmosphere here is always that of quiet and calm
—no one could disturb this.
And though the people are the only real threat,
they are all too well trained and aware
to ever introduce the least clumsiness
or disturbing element into the room.

At times it is hard to believe
what is before one's eyes—
there is no answer to this except the room itself,
and maybe the white clouds seen through the window.

No one in the house was sure of the frontiers
and the beautiful atlas gilded and bound with blue silk
was only of antiquarian interest and quite useless
for the new questions. The whole situation
was like a painting within a painting and
that within another and so on and so on—
until everyone had lost sight of their original landmarks.
The heath melted into the sky on the horizon.
And the questions of definition and contrast
only brought on a series of fruitless searches
and examinations that made everyone irritable and exhausted.

Once the surveyors had abandoned their project
the objects once more took over.
It would be false to deny the sigh of relief
there was when this happened and calm returned.

The bus bumped down the avenue
and ahead were the mountains and the woods
that burst into flower as spring settled.
The plan and the heavy revolver were all quite in keeping
with this, despite the apparent superficial
difference and clash of worlds—
there was really only one world.
It wasn't easy—admittedly—and someone
had to stay behind and . . .
The word in the sky had slowly dissolved
and was now nowhere to be seen.
But instead the sun was flooding the whole room
and everything took on a golden aura
—this meant we were even aware of the
band of horsemen now riding through the forest
that surrounded the valley.

The many details may appear evasive
but the purpose of the total was obvious
and uncompromising

SOFT WHITE

When the sea is as grey as her eyes
On these days for sure   the soft white
mist blown in from the ocean   the town dissolving
It all adds up   her bare shoulders

Nakedness   rolling in from the sea
on winter afternoons   a fine rain
looking down on the sand   and shingle
the waves breaking on the shore   and white

It is impossible to deny what
taken by surprise   then wonder
the many details of her body
to be held first now   then later

In body and mind   the fine rain outside
on winter afternoons   the nakedness
of her bare shoulders   as grey as her eyes
the sea rushing up the beach as white as

The whole outline called "geography"
meeting at a set of erotic points
lips   shoulders   breasts   stomach
the town dissolves   sex   thighs   legs

Outside   then across her nakedness
it rains in the afternoon   then the wonder
her body so young and firm   dissolves the town
in winter   grey as her eyes

THIS YEAR

The children playing on the front step
the sea is green
today   the power games
can't be gentler

The walk along the beach at night
shingle   back home the animals
all playing games underlined with violence
maybe cruelty

Everyone gets very religious
this year   it even opens out
but the desire to give out messages
has to be suppressed in favour of

A neat square is moist and green
its trees each have their
thin black branches that glisten with water
found by accident   it's very warming

To be here   the sea is green
at times grey   there are two empty houses
in the neat square   the windows   a black enamel
Surprised

As she undresses   the children playing in the street
the sea is green   her young body womanly
loose clothes hid her great beauty
at times grey   "olive" she said

Everyone gets very religious
I can understand why   even the power games
gentler   when play stops
what then?   gentler   surprised

Undressed   it's very warming
her young breasts fuller than   no messages
in favour of   nor against
her nipples are small and a defeating pink

Today   green power games can be
gentler than the sea   on the beach
shoo the animals   your lap
her beauty undresses   the sea

LINEN

waking on the purple sheets whose softness
The streets heavy with summer   the night thick with green leaves
drifting into sleep we lay
The dazzle of morning   the hot pavements
fruit markets   "The Avenues"

"You and I are pretty as the morning"

on the beaches
machine-gunning the fleeing army
the fighters coming in low "at zero"
the sun behind them   and bombs falling all round
"Jah Jah"   CLICK CLICK   "Jah Jah"

the cheap pages crumbling already after so little time
St. Petersburg renamed the Soviet Printing House maybe

you leave the town   "the softness" like a banner
though where
In the countryside the trees bare and scrub bushes
scattered in useless fields
the darkness of a stand of larches
called "the dark woods" on no map

touching you   like the
and soft as
like the scent of flowers and
like an approaching festival
whose promise is failed through carelessness

ANIMAL DAYS

1

"The polo season would start early in April
so there was no time to be wasted."

the night growing darker   the black plains
and below   the bright lights of the town

"knights on horses"?   "gentle ladies"?   "towers in the forest"?

it was as though your eyes filled with glass tears
crying some strange

there were peacocks on the high balconies
and a golden light   in fact "a heavenly rod"
came down from the heart of a clear blue sky
you see

2

"You're right, even though you won't accept it."

. . . with all the rifles brought back to safety
even the glimmer of polished metal

Buzzards, kestrels and hawks
circling high above the valley

the dust of the road   dazzling
with the white gates shut   do you understand
the garden so enclosed, and too green?

3

food is so very good

it is very black these days

the malevolence on the winter island

and what approaches in the darkness

beyond all knowledge   "the endurance"
surviving the fear

"but we're all so afraid"

and the children?

the indian chiefs
what are the wounds, anyway, and their cost?

In the morning everything is white
low clouds trail across the upper pastures
and the valley is thick with mist

"sometimes their canoes only hollowed-out tree trunks"

4

standing in the shadows or maybe in the distance
he   Like a long arcade or cloister
It was far from the grim scenes of the north
In his red tunic

The morning spent loading cord-wood onto a trailer

five young foxes in the bean-field waiting for the wood-pigeons

in the beech woods up on the ridge—the bark
still green and wet, the "sticks" just felled.

It's reduced to a violent struggle
with heavy machinery, and boredom

the castle crumbling sedately   "damn fool!"
the gilding already flaking off

Cutting it up into "blocks "on the saw-bench
The forest floor all torn up with bulldozer tracks
the soil a bright red   exposed below
the white shale backbone of the ridge

the sun sinking lower
the whole forest dripping moisture and green

the old railway station

5

holding a young rabbit in my hands
walking across the stubble in the late afternoon

soft fur   shocking like the heart-beat

the dark river   and angry knights milling
in the courtyard

setting it free in a hawthorn thicket
safe from the dogs

at night the land so bare   "rustles"

"They have no tradition of keeping their colonies neat."

"I care for that woman" the song began

6

squandered in a matter called "the heat of the moment"
not knowing what

". . . at dusk the sound of church bells from the valley floor,
an owl flying low over a passing tractor."

white with rain

The corrugated-iron roof of the mission discoloured
with rust   the deep green of the jungle
in the humid gorge

Like oppressors   striking fear into people
with threats of pillage and "no quarter"

Inside the walls where
"No!"
too heavy   on evenings like this

in the courtyard
"the battlements"

Today

I tidy the room
it all becomes a notebook or an excuse

> "A bay seen through the window—it's a
> summer morning—the romantic coaster ploughs on
> leaving a smoky trail behind.
> At sea : 6 bells."

From the window : cluttered back-yards

It's now down to a matter of lists
that act as buttresses, even defences.
No? the same tired and selfish stories?

Out there . . .

There seems to be great activity
and everyone has been invited to collaborate
It's all very curious and useless
I mean "what body winds round what body?"
a poor excuse for "intellectual search"
or "a full and active life"—
though at times being "in love" is a life in itself

The floor is swept and all the ledges meticulously dusted
the room is then well aired by opening the window wide
I'm left standing in the middle of the room
holding a wet cloth

There are too many accounts of cruelties
but the other side always sounds slightly false
or is an expression of nostalgia
But what can ache more than repetition?

Cut into slices?
Stuck in *"the vertical"*—is that too obscure?

THE LONG BLACK VEIL :
a notebook 1970-72

"things have ends (or scopes) and beginnings. To
know what precedes   and what follows
*   will assist yr / comprehension of process"*

Ezra Pound—*Canto 77*

"In the Congo what joy could I take in gathering unknown flowers with no one
to whom to give them?"

André Gide—*Journals, 31 March 1930*

PREFACE

How to accept
this drift

the move   not mapped
nor clear other than in
its existence

a year passed
I think of you
it's early on a sunny morning in June
and think of your thinking of me
possible

How do we live with this?
yet live with this

What have we *left*
from all *this*?

        "Concepts promise protection
from experience.
                The spirit does
not dwell in concepts. Oh Jung."
                (Joanne Kyger—*'Desecheo Notebook'*)

two years passed "Oh Jung"
the cycle not repeated
only the insistence

The story is that, when a child, Borges used to come to his father. His father would have a number of coins that he would place on his desk one by one, one on top of the other. To be brief—the stack of coins is an image of how our memory distorts and simplifies events the farther we move from them. The first coin is the actual event, the next coin is the event recreated in the mind, the memory, the next coin is a recreation of the first recreation, etc., etc., . . .

But what of the essence of this? "Oh Jung's" insistences. The Sufi story of the famous River that tried to cross the desert, but only crossed the sands as water "in the arms of the wind", nameless but

BOOK ONE

the soft dawn   it's light
I mean your body   and how I ache now
yes, tremble
                    the words?   how can they . . .

somehow the raven flying through endless skies
that ache too much   the unbearable distance
borne

Across the valley the sun catches the white silos
of these scattered farms
Up on the ridge

I mean following the creek . . .

As we lie in each other
dazed and hanging like birds on the wind

your body, yes   I'm talking about it
at last   I mean this *is* the discovery
Need I list the items?

On your way from the thorn tree to the house
you stop and half turn
to tell me . . .
that doesn't matter
but your look
and this picture I have
and at this distance

I have this now
I have what I have
                    in my hands

dawn—light—body—words—raven—skies—ache—distance
—valley—sun—silos—farms—ridge—creek—each other—birds—wind

The Flight—BA 591

Book Two

Baseball in Central Park.
Anti-war parade on 5th Avenue.
The Egyptian rooms in the Metropolitan.
Reading Gide's "Journals" in my room.

On the bus : the green Catskills. large black birds standing in the grass.
wild blue iris in the swamps. two woodchucks. two rabbits. If other
men's shoes fit, wear 'em.

We swim naked in the pool at night. The stars so bright. The hot night,
the crickets and frogs singing. I hold you to me in a small room—the
night air so heavy. Inside "the dream" . . .

A farm dog barks somewhere across the valley.

The bright greens of the woods, the sun streaming down through the
branches. The crashings of a chicken hawk suddenly startled and flying
up through the branches to the safety of the sky again. The rain that
increases and

thunder in the distance
the air heavy
and the valley white with mist

our bodies wet

As dawn breaks
we wake
and make love
again
the sky grey outside
and the birds singing

The sun comes up
You rise and make coffee
The woods so green

We go back to bed and

I can hear your footsteps
going about the house
doing things
while I sit by the window
of this upstairs room

the birds singing
in the heavy afternoon
the muffled sounds of a t.v.
downstairs

that I want you
this is why

I will call anything that goes on in my head "a dream", whether it be
thoughts or imaginings, day-dreams or sleep dreams. They all give
pictures of "the possible", and that is exactly their value.

the two warships ploughed out to sea
waves flowed between them
as though dolphins lovingly touched each hull
in turn   No flecks of dust on the captain's
fine uniform   All the brass polished

Not the first   but one of many
such expeditions

Book Three

1:00pm, check into the hotel. It has two rooms and a bar. The town has two stores, three bars, a post office, church, gas station, fire station, and a small country library. People drive into town in their pick-up trucks, but it's not *that* "country".

Evening time out on the front porch step, smoking a cigar, watching the cars and people pass. Night bugs flying round the lights. Young men driving in pegs, putting up tents back of the fire station ready for the weekend "Fire Department Chicken Fry". The hot heavy night bringing the thunder and warm rain. Go to bed, the noise of passing trucks and the juke-box downstairs.

The fascination with *this* formality, *this* ritual.

Woken up early in the morning by the thunder, and rain beating on the tin roof of the porch. When I get up the air so soft and sweet. The square and hillsides a soft white with the fine mist. In the bar local farmers and workers from the nearby steel mills talking—". . . a nigger wench, not a nigger woman . . ." As I leave the sun breaks through on to the lush greenness of this valley.

Walk up the ridge west of the town—the minnows darting in the creek. The rock bed, and the currents there. The smell of young ferns as I walk up the hill through the beech woods.

Go up to the wild strawberry patch again, squat down and eat some. Continue up along the road, the pine woods by the crest of the ridge "see for miles"

You walk through the door
No, now you stop your car in a small town square
I get up from the porch step and greet you
This is all "country manners"

There's no steamer bringing you to me
up-river at the hill-station
No long white dress on the verandah

It is . . .
I hold you.   Isn't this enough?
The feel of your breasts
          beneath your loose white shirt

"It was used by the commentator of the Himyarite Ode, either at first
hand or through the medium of Hamdani's *Iklil*. We may regard it,
like the commentary itself, as a historical romance in which most of
the characters and some of the events are real, adorned with fairy-tales,
fictitious verses, and such entertaining matter as a man of learning and
storyteller by trade might naturally be expected to introduce. Among the
few remaining Muhammadan authors who bestowed special attention
on the Pre-Islamic period of South Arabian history, I shall mention here
only Hamza of Isfahan, the eighth book of whose *Annals* (finished in 961
A.D.) provides a useful sketch, with brief chronological details, of the
Tubba's or Himyarite kings of Yemen."

          (R. A. Nicholson—'A *Literary History of The Arabs*')

The small town set in a valley winding between ridges,
the lush green, the white mist at dawn,
the creek bed almost dry,
white scattered boulders and the willows.
The meadows so deep, and floating on their surface
the yellow and orange flowers.
The cool beech woods on late afternoons.
You melt into this landscape
and this only a description of my love for you

At the hill-station   all the bearers fled

The delighted naturalist was left unconcerned
carefully placing his specimens in the black metal box

". . . and when he spoke about it to his friends they smiled and said they
found the comparison odd, but they immediately dropped the subject
and went on to talk about something else. Hebdomeros concluded from
this that perhaps they had not really understood what he meant, and
he reflected on the difficulty of making oneself understood when one's
thoughts reached a certain height or depth. 'It's strange,' Hebdomeros
was thinking, 'as for me, the very idea that something had escaped

my understanding would keep me awake at nights, whereas people in general are not in the least perturbed when they see or read or hear things they find completely obscure.'"

(Giorgio de Chirico—*Hebdomeros)*

Book Four

We choose our condition

the sun shines
the warmth and softness of your flesh
"belly to belly" (like the song says)

The air so clear up on the ridge
this light
and then looking down to the valley

"our condition chooses us"
she says

In the morning we go for a drive, buy cakes and
milk, and picnic by the creek. The afternoon
spent in the meadow. In the evening we make love
in the room.

the sun glittering   through the glass
scattering rainbows on the walls and ceiling
the soft turf beneath the trees outside
your room where we lie naked
with our love

the country music plays
the words sung
"Palms of victory, crowns of glory.
   Palms of victory I shall wear."

. . . felt so good this morning—as though I woke up beside you.

Book Five : Canadian Days

On the Northlands train from Toronto up to North Bay, Cochrane, and Kapuskasing. Then bus onto Hearst ("Moose Capital of the North"), and a jeep ride out to Jogues.
The night before the train full of drunks and bear hunters. Ridiculous. "No guffing".

And today early morning, the grey dawn. The "towns" we stop at just a collection of huts scattered at random around the rail halt and a dirt road. And then the bush again. Heavy streams and rivers, and the forest cluttered with dead and fallen trees. The occasional windswept meadow, a grey weathered farmhouse deserted, fallen apart. Nothing. The bleak empty plain, marsh, lakes, the crowded conifer woods, a single silver birch in the middle of this.

The Northlands. The watery sunlight on dirt roads. The dull green country. Hardly any flowers to be seen.

At night the stars brighter than I'd ever seen them, and the curtains of light, the Aurora Borealis. This brightness dazzling, but it's with you that I want it.

It is the surface
your eyes
The foresters tramp in weary
Driven into a corner (so to speak)
to say this
I hold your head between my hands
your eyes

In the morning sitting on the front step, everything so calm and still. The warm sun, and a total quiet only broken by the bark of the ravens. The vast blue sky, and the forest stretching off on all sides. The long straight white dirt roads with a line of telegraph poles along side, and then the forest enclosing them on either side.

Book Six

The questions of complexity

On Gide's death Mr. Forster said—"I realized more clearly how much he had got out of life, and had managed to transmit through his writings. Not life's greatness—greatness is a nineteenth century perquisite, a Goethean job. But life's complexity, and the delight, the difficulty, the duty of registering that complexity and of conveying it."

The distinctions

"Oh, Jung" (1875-1961) on "Marriage . . ." (1925)

The container *and* the contained
not *or*

one within the other
a continual shifting   and that both ways
—more a flow—from the simplicity to the complexity,
"unconscious" to conscious,
                          and then back again?
and the move always with difficulty, and pain   a pleasure

not so much a repetition
but a moving around a point, a line
—like a backbone—and that too moving
(on)

yang and yin
light and dark

An island set among islands
and that no answer
But the need there—
somehow to have all one's hopes there,
to see and touch, to be wholly in one place.
Yet over the horizon   as real as any . . .
the ghosts
and them always moving

BEFORE COMPLETION   Wei Chi / 64
But if the little fox, after nearly completing the crossing
Gets his tail in the water,
There is nothing that would further.

                        in the half light . . .
A minotaur? a cat? tiger?   Her face
a metamorphosis   seen   at once   many times.
Our powers generating . . .
We touch, hold, and caress ourself

A bird flying high in the sky
above the clouds, and below them
an ocean, and a ship moving there.

"Such thoughts were very far from Julien's mind. His love was still
another name for ambition. It meant for him the joy of possessing so
beautiful a woman, when he himself was a poor, unhappy creature
whom men despised. His acts of adoration, and his rapture at the sight
of his mistress's charms, ended by reassuring Madame de Rênal on the
question of the difference in their ages. Had she possessed a little of that
practical knowledge of the world which in the most civilized countries
a woman of thirty has had at her disposal for a number of years already,
she might have trembled for the duration of a love which apparently
only existed on surprise and the transports of gratified self-esteem."

(Stendhal—*Le rouge et le noir*)

Book Seven

My stomach   burns   Coming to you

How will . . . ?

The peaceful and flowering public gardens,
the smell of the ocean again
So much tied in such sites
of past pleasures

Stepping into the new   always   with you

A low haze beyond the harbour's mouth

I am full and happy   now   at your side

. . . we finally begin to fall asleep as dawn comes,
as a single whippoorwill starts to sing . . .

we wake, and make love. Outside a grey sea mist fills the woods. Later,
standing alone in these woods waiting for her, not knowing how . . . this
journey today so far from

The tricks are pulled

         blue skies flash across the screen

The falsity when anything becomes a symbol

You are lowered   very gently
into the waiting boat alongside

Much later   ashore on this island
where tears rarely happen . . .

You are away there on other continents
So hard—"It is hard to stand firm in the middle"
—waiting   for that lightness, that ease
of movement

The freighter was anchored in the middle of the bay with a full head of steam up. As the launch approached

In the Museum of Fine Arts, Boston—

> *Mycerinus and his queen, Khamerernebty II*
> slate. fourth dynasty (2613-2494 B.C.)
> (The Pharaoh Mycerinus also known as Menkaure.)

In the Egyptian Museum, Cairo—

> *Mycerinus triad : Mycerinus, Hathor, and the*
> *personification of the "Dog" nome.*
> slate. fourth dynasty.
> (The personification of the "Dog" district
> (nome) is a woman.)

the tenderness. They stand facing us, she to his left, her right arm around his waist, her left hand resting on his left upper arm.

Horus, Hathor, Anubis

Horus—the falcon headed god, the sun.

Hathor—the cow headed goddess, the sky.

Anubis—the jackal headed god, the guardian of the dead.

Horus, the rising sun, enters Hathor, the sky.
Obvious enough.

Doors flung open, a clear blue day outside, cactus, sage brush, and the yellow desert ochre, and the blue sky.   New Mexico.

Horus, son of Osiris, a falcon, whose two eyes are the sun and the moon, and whose breath is the cooling north wind.

Hathor, the cow, the sky goddess, stars on her belly, the sun between her horns, guardian of the Western Mountain, goddess of the copper mines of Sinai, of a woman's love and joy, of perfumes and spices, identified by the Greeks as Aphrodite. The mother who gives birth to Ra, the sun, at dawn. The destroyer on whose back Ra rides through the sky.

Anubis, the jackal, guardian of the desert cemeteries, master of embalmment, who oversees the weighing of each heart.

"a god is power personified . . . In Egypt . . ."

No godhead, no gospel, but "a multiplicity of approaches", each in its own right, each immanent in nature.

Book Eight : England

So much either side of the immediate
though at its height—the love ecstasy
of the "now"—it is only the immediate,
God's face.
(the Sufi poet, Ibn 'Arabi, writes of this)
God's face is the face of your lover.

I love you

the sky is full of wheeling gulls
Do I ask too much?
—the sea crashing white on the shingle—
that I'm torn apart each time you leave

the white buildings
the green sea and hills behind the town,
like some giant sandwich
and our love in the filling of it

You wheel above me

such whiteness

Christ, that I love you

how to deal with this?

I wait for you
not passively   but
I wait for you

My heart weeps

Who would ever have thought I'd write that?
"My heart weeps"?

"You must try, Psyche, to use up all your facility against an obstacle; face the granite, rouse yourself against it, and for a while despair. See your vain enthusiasms and your frustrated aims fall away. Perhaps you lack sufficient wisdom yet to prefer your will to your ease. You find that stone too hard, you dream of the softness of wax and the obedience of clay? Follow the path of your aroused thought and you will soon meet this infernal inscription: *There is nothing so beautiful as that which does not exist.*"

(Paul Valéry—'Concerning Adonis')

Not a climbing, but a moving across the surface in a certain way, as though a soaking into the grain, what was there all the time, though never fully realised.

As though a monster haunts us—continually aroused at each "wrong" word, each "wrong" action, and roaring out from its darkness to terrorize us again. A giant and indestructible serpent filled with anger and venom, nightmare.

"Each single angel is terrifying." (Rilke)

Summer. The water meadows at dusk. The willows and long grass either side of the winding river, now only seen as a smooth black surface, the flow imperceptible. The buttercups indistinguishable in the growing darkness. Only the sound of your feet on the narrow gravel path. A cuckoo in a nearby spinney. The swallows out hunting. Across the fields the dim outline of the town—a clock strikes the hour, maybe in the church or the marketplace.

BOOK NINE

Today, lying on the grass in the park
by your house
                      We were very close
Your husband, your children, you go
about your duties, you love
and care for them

Yes.

you there
me here

sometimes it's an ocean
spread between our bodies
sometimes only a matter of
yards across a carpeted room

you sit there
I sit here
there are people around us

the luxury
of setting eyes on you

You walk by my side through the park
what luxury
the

the cars the planes
the absurd mechanics
when all I want
is to walk up the hill to you

the silly girls clatter round
while you—the only woman I know,
the only woman I want—
are kept so securely from me
and at such a distance

a fierce wind tugs at the town
while I walk up the hill
and you on the other shore
while the sea bursts on this shore

there is a fine rain—I repeat myself—
it's night   there is a wind
To answer to . . . ?
when our world turns in us
dazzling
That hand offered us when the clouds part

"No, it's real,
it's what I feel."
                    (by 'The Soft Machine')

The pride. Being with you, knowing very simply where I'm going, where I stand, of being able to put aside all the half-things and live with one sure knowledge of what matters, what is.

". . . an ease in the air around us that we can spread into . . . and ideas are like stars instead of gravity—we're not held by them by their necessities."
                    (your letter)

Book Ten

The rain falling you could be driving a car now
somewhere

You drive the car and my hand rests on your shoulder
the radio is playing
the rain is beating on the car roof
and the road is a brilliant black

the honour of you
"I am honoured" someone says

that I should cry now

we all know what this means
and there's no need for any rich details

when John said "from egotistical to egocentric"
he was right about the process
there's no cause for shame

and the "honour"?

the word grows emptier the farther it moves
from the flesh
while *my* honour lives in your flesh

"You're your own train, you got your own track, and you can go
anywhere."

(Fielding Dawson quoting Charles Olson in
                                    'The Black Mountain Book')

But you the ground,
earth I want,
the place

the luxury of it
to hold my reality in my arms

the touch
of it
you
the feel of you
so much now

BOOK ELEVEN

Is it the Rilkean dream or "home" we come to?
At dusk the skyline obscure.
Yes and No.

Many pictures—the surface apparently the same.
A series of events, but the marks they leave varying.   Things
happen, have qualities.

And ahead?
The mountains, the wind, the sea   are there
we move through them, across their surfaces

like a moving hunter

On a "threshold"?   in the open
dazzled by the sunlight, and "nervous",

but moving—and that with care.
No end.

But the quality

The dreams do happen—
and there is no "home" we come to
—but on this earth, and open to its powers

A recognition of the ghosts that guide us. The dead watching over us,
surrounding us with a tenderness—as though they were gravity—they
hold us, their arms around us, however we move.

And Anubis guiding the dead through their journey.
Before the tribunal of Osiris, Anubis, the jackal-headed god, watches
over the weighing of the dead man's heart—the heart in one scale, and
in the other an ostrich feather, symbol of Ma'at, the goddess of truth.
And if the heart is truthful the dead man is led up to Osiris by Anubis
and becomes Osiris, god of the dead, of the under world—that is, of the
earth beneath our feet.

the eucalyptus groves on the mountain sides the road cuts
through—no—follows the contour obediently. The coast . . .

the heat and wetness of us

later alone on the beach . . .　　the sandpipers rush about,
following each wave out, picking the sand. The gulls

. . . through the barrier. "That isn't pain, it's something else."

driving through the mountains. San Anselmo. San Rafael. the redwoods. The ease of walking in the hot sun in California down a dirt path laughing, ordering milk-shakes, and watching the traffic pass. Of being totally in one place. The dry mountains around us. Nowhere else

At night the smell of orange blossom at the post-office

In the bar I talked with this man passing through town about Union matters.

". . . For Beauty's nothing
but the beginning of Terror we're still just able to bear,
and we adore it so because it serenely
disdains to destroy us. Each single angel is terrifying.

Ein jeder Engel ist schrecklich."

(Rilke—'Duino Elegies' 1)

walk the length of the beach as far as the rocks watching the small and large sandpipers. Orange butterflies glide above the parking lot.

when we're together the time always so short. The minutes counted and noted down. And around these times the long hours of waiting.

that hot surface where our bodies meet, press together—"a melting spot".

she tells me of

the tearing

leaving

the only woman

We drive up into the mountains behind the beach. Muir Woods. Mount Tamalpais. The air so clear and sweet. On the short turf . . . her laughing. She looks so beautiful.

In the evening in the room . . .

Making love, the final blocks clear. My body taken into her body completely, and then her body into my body.

In that place the ease there

more beautiful than ever, her black hair so thick and rich

She anoints my wrists

the anointment a ritual like the sweetening of the body before burial, before our parting. My not realising the completeness of this until now.

In the distance the mountains—the dream echoed again and again in many parts, in many places. An antelope (not understanding this animal) lies down exhausted yet calm. Some form of quietness.

The ritual of—repeated again—No. We make love—to each other—in turn. The body glowing, dizzy, . . . walking through clouds. The faces transformed again.

She accepts the objects—the stone, the orange blossom.
She gives the objects—the whittled twig, the dried seed pod

She puts the bead bracelet around my wrist

                                    lie naked upon the bed.

ONE, TWO, THREE

An emperor gives a gift, stylishly,
and a Mughal miniature records it
(colour and gold on paper, height 7 3/16 inches)

we're dazzled — all this art
and surprises   "Keeping the doors open"
Right?

Yes, I suppose, fascinated by the delicacy
of the piano part in the first movement
of Beethoven's "Ghost" Trio
("he sighed . . ."   but real enough,
aesthetic coat-trailing aside.
The delight beyond the technicalities
—not pursuing, but there
to be recognised

We can see this

And all those private separations?

When "we" moves from the general
to the particular?

To talk of *you* now . . . ?
amongst all this "delight"
—moving into that other level—
the poverty of this, one without the other,
the delight more a refuge than any whole thing
when you're away

Up in the hills the court is assembled,
the gifts exchanged
From the balcony I see you cross a courtyard,
could almost touch you—
but the distance.
                    Be well.

the moonlight on your face
as you sleep now

★ ★ ★

hold me

outside the rain falling in the street
I hold you   your flesh so soft

to begin to say—"I love you . . ."?

the heat of your belly

away   the hills
(Fuck "the hills")

my mouth on your throat
my body smells of your body

★ ★ ★

There are many fields
and the fortresses are so far apart.
The troops stand in line on the parade ground
while the sun beats down on them
and their bored officers.

it's another day

meanwhile . . .

                              there are many settings

A group of men can sit stiffly
for a regimental photo of the survivors of the disaster,
and then try to look neat and alert.

And their children . . . ?
living in a calm beyond this knowledge?
It is not so much a question of guilt
on either side, but maybe some form of recognition
which rarely happens.

And the years pass until one generation dies
and their knowledge with them
leaving behind only feelings of confused longing
that quietly spread beyond any conscious resentment.

Now put it together.

BRIGHTON • OCTOBER

a cloud passes by
the stuffed animals in the museum
    continue to stare straight ahead

at sea three freighters wait on the tide
    to enter the small port

load of timber
cargo of coal

a man walks along the edge of a park
beneath the trees that have just begun
to shed their leaves

I am thinking of the forms of peace,
or, rather, pure pleasure

Old Bosham Bird Watch

for Jud

1

out of nothing comes . . .

nothing comes out of nothing

cut   /   switch to

a small room, in a building of small rooms. "Enclosed thus." Outside there are bare trees groaning and twisting in the wind. A cold long road with houses either side that finally leads down hill to a railway station. The Exit.

2

Out on the estuary four people in a small dinghy at high tide. Canada geese and oyster catchers around. The pale winter sunlight and cold clear air. Onshore the village church contains the tomb of Canute's daughter, the black Sussex raven emblazoned on the stone. Small rooms.

3

Sat round a fire. The black Danish raven rampant.
In the dream.
Enclosed, I reach out. She moves in her ways that the facts of closeness, familiarity, obscure. Our not quite knowing one another in that sense of clear distance, that sense that comes with distance, like old photos making everything so set, clear, and easily understood—so we think.
Face to face the changes flicking by second by second. Not the face fixed that yes I know her. Not the easy sum of qualities

4

How long since you've known who you are? How long? Why who you? Don't know. Long time. Only have old photos, old images, old ikons peeling. That man who lived at X, did Y, travelled to Z, and back, "The Lone Gent"?
Why, who was that masked man? Why, don't you know?
NO!

5

In the closeness that comes with shared actions. From keeping a room clean, keeping clothes clean, cooking a meal to be eaten by the both of us. In that closeness, maybe on the edge of losing something gaining something. Questions of clarity and recognitions.

6

We swing hard a-port then let the current take us, the ebb tide pulling us out towards the Channel. The birds about, the colours of the sky, the waters, all the different plants growing beside the estuary, and the heavy brown ploughed fields behind these banks. Here, more than anywhere else, every thing, all becomes beautiful and exciting—and the fact of being alive at such moments, being filled with this immense beauty, right, Rilke, "ecstasy", makes the fact of living immeasurably precious.

7

Enclosed by cold in the winter. The clear sharp days walking down hill looking out to sea, the wind up, the waves crashing on the shingle beaches. And the days of rain and harsh grey skies, coming home from work in the dark through the car lights and shop lights. The exit always there. I can't say I "know" you. But neither can I say what "knowing" is. We are here, and somehow it works, our being together.

8

The sky, the gulls wheeling and squawking above, the flint walls of these South Saxon churches, the yew trees branching up into that winter sky. I know these. But not what you're thinking, what anyone is thinking. I can never know that, only work with that—as it comes. Open arms open air come clear.

9

The dinghy is brought ashore. The people drag it up the bank and carry it to the cottage where they stow it neatly. Everything "ship shape". Out to sea the coasters head for Shoreham and Newhaven. Along the coast small blue trains rattle along through Chichester, Littlehampton, Worthing, and on to Brighton.
The fire is stoked up in the small room. The people in the cottage all eat dinner together, are happy in one another's company.
That I love you, we know this, parting the branches and ferns as we push on through the wood.

CHÊN 震

one of those
        rare
                moments
      when

thoughts of death
strike

The desire to hang on
      to what
           I have

to not   lose
sight
      of
          what's held dear
the line of hills
          that edge
(the) coast

*

sometimes there is

the need

    to explain

make that mark

        clear

the clarity

    what believed

or rather   hoped for

*

        to be afraid   of

no action clear

    but

      sets of blocks

the hard rain at night

but with mornings

      (so) clear

blue sky and sun

like spring   the winter

to move carefully

        here

      but how

when so crowded

        by those fears

*

Chên / the arousing (51)

"When a man has learned within his
heart what fear and trembling mean,
he is safeguarded against any terror
produced by outside influences."

"Six in the fifth place means:

Shock goes hither and thither.

Danger.

However, nothing at all is lost.

Yet there are things to be done."

★

fear, v.i. & t. : to be afraid of,
hesitate to do, shrink from doing;
revere.

★

"a long road"

                    she said

"it's a long road"

fear of loss

the loss spreads   (as much)

through the future

            as in the past

Hauntings

     in the face of which

           we

survive somehow

"a long road"

You essai. You o.k.

for Paul Evans

> "Once again, the philosophy of darkness
> will dissolve above the dazzling sea."
>
> Albert Camus 1948

1

a rock outcrop in the sea

a deserted car standing on the empty shore road

Gulls shriek in the air above the rock
while below thrift and small orchids flower
in that awesome hush between the waves breaking

The blue leather upholstery of the car is too hot to touch
the sun being that bright and strong today
A neat green cardboard box has been placed on the back seat

The scents of the sea and the coast join
somewhere up there in the sky—
                    A pyramid of light?

Or would you be bored by all this after the first day?
The ground too damp and civilisation too far away?
What if it rains and you have to trudge miles to the nearest shop or pub
or public transport to get away from all this, to have a few decent 'home
comforts'?

2 /1900/

Hold the horses! It's Hotel Wolf!
or as they now say, in these modern times,
Wolf Hotel, and since then renamed The Sisson,
Saratoga, Wyoming.

Step inside
to the palm filled lounge and big easy chairs
and just the right soupçon of barbarism.

O cold blooded murderers,
the sweet-hearts and glory of this continent!

"Peaches! Fresh peaches!" cried the two gauchos,
and the little boy, lifting the canvas that covered their fruit cart,
saw only a heap of severed heads.

You do step into the bar, but are rightly nervous beneath your assured
and sporty manner. No tennis courts here, I'm sorry to say, only child-
like card-games played by unpleasant adults. I wouldn't stay long if I
were you, though I'm not.

3

I turn my back on all that and re-enter
the alchemist's dark chambers
A glass prism is set on the table top
beneath the window and scatters sunlight
in bands of colour 'a marvel to behold'

Books, equipment, and implements are
stacked about the room
all as aids to discover 'the wonders and secrets of nature'
through human invention and curiosity
godlike

a stuffed baby crocodile hangs from the ceiling
the retort glows gold with its fire

Dear Sir,

Your moods of deep depression can weigh heavily on you for several days or more. I can really do very little for you or your state. Such melancholy can take up to 6 years to fade from your heart after the original emotional shock. I would suggest your taking long walks in the countryside and that you try to mix socially as much as is possible.

Signed,

a doctor.

4

TO SPELL IT OUT: the barbarity in all its forms,
in the face of which our blundering frailty,
our frail giant-steps.

"This book," wrote the French Resistance leader Colonel Georges, "springs from a sadness and a certain amount of disgust at seeing myths take so much precedence over history . . . Our truth has no need of mirrors that would exaggerate it."*

And you, Anna, with your two fierce-looking sisters and, presumably, stories of real hardships and dangers in the now placid Mid-West, or even further west, Kansas maybe. It's different somehow, though I can't explain.

Families on all sides of 'The Water', with their own strengths like islands in the flood, us all sat on top of the roof like a bunch of drenched chickens waiting for the waters to subside and then be submerged again within the family.
It's difficult to explain, warming and frightening at the same time, the love there.

There are the Grand Events, the 'dangerous times' when maybe more than a rightness about a family is needed—though I can't say we live in such times, and, even so, any such dramatic behaviour has to have a base-camp somewhere, n'est-ce pas?   though maybe not

* Colonel Georges (Robert Noireau)—*Le Temps des Partisans.*

5

Paul, you must know it already, but how in the upper left margin of the first page of the manuscript score for *The Fourth of July,* Charles Ives wrote to his copyist—

> "Mr. Price: Please don't try to make things nice! All the wrong notes are right. Just copy as I have. I want it that way."

You walk by the sea on a grey February afternoon with your daughter Lucy and a grossly over-enthusiastic dog. On our meeting we remember, though don't talk of it, the obviously lucid and witty conversation we'd had the night before when (somewhat) the worse for drink!

The mistakes, the difficulties, . . . these words almost used too much so that they become some sort of totem or excuse, but it all falling, and us too, every whichaway.

In a little frequented corner of the museum we find an old and heavily embroidered trade union banner on display. The gold silk on a dark red velvet background shows a motif of clasped hands, and all of this faded and somewhat the worse for wear too. I can't make out the motto, but it's probably something like "Strength in Unity" or . . .

Out in the street again we head back towards the beach. The sea really *is* magnificent, a vast sweep of silver-shot slate grey that fades off and up into the white grey of the sky. The chilling sea wind grips our bones.

CLARET LABEL

The large grey château isolated in the middle of lawns and pastures that extend beyond reason.

A large dark grey building put to the cruel uses its exterior already suggests.

A Gestapo Headquarters—interrogation rooms and cells—the top window on the left almost exactly half way between the end of the building and the main entrance.

Though this is in my imagination in a sun-filled kitchen in the early afternoon in September

where such interrogations could equally happen—husband and wife piling up cruelly logical absurdities, complaints, and accusations while the babies cry in the next room.

Monsters & Co.

The top window on the left of a slum tenement seen from a train window passing through east London—Bethnal Green, Stratford . . .

Stop the train. Step into that room. "Hello, I am Anthony Barnett, Norway's greatest jazz xylophone player. I saw you through the window. I saw you moving about your room, sitting watching t.v.. I had to come to say 'hello', to embrace you. We humans must stick together."

The film breaks at this point. Crackling noises and smoke pour from the improvised projection room. The village priest rushes out threatening the noisy audience to be quiet or else . . . If we sit quiet and still we will be allowed to see the rest of *Sabu the Elephant Boy* with French sub-titles.

A POEM FOR WRITERS

To finally pull the plug on the word machine,
to rise from the chair late one evening
and step back into the quiet and darkness?

The dull white lights of the control-room of
a large hydro-electric dam in Russia
a computer centre in Brighton
the bridge of a giant oil tanker in the Indian Ocean.
Subdued light that reaches every corner
with no variation, tone, or shadow.

To leave the warm desk-light's tent
and step out into the . . .
        "I am just going outside and may be some time, Scottie"

Trains rush through the night,
across country through suburbs past factories oil refineries dumps,
the lights from their windows quickly disturbing the dark fields and woods
or the railway clutter as they pass through town,
staring in at the bare rooms and kitchens
each lit with its own story that lasts for years and years.
A whole zig-zag path, and the words stumble and fidget
around what has happened.

To walk out one January morning across the Downs
a low mist on the hills and the furrows coated with frost,
the dew ponds iced up.
The cold dry air.
And the sudden excitement when a flock of partridges starts up
in front of you and whirrs off and down to the left,
skimming the freshly ploughed fields.

"O ma blessure" groan the trees
with the wounds of a multitude of small boys' penknives.

No, not that—
but the land, the musics, the books
always attendant

amongst the foolish rush and scramble for vainglory,
talk or noise for its own sake, a semblance of energy
but not necessity.

Throw your cap in the air, get on your bike, and pedal off
down hill—it's a joy with no need of chatter,
Hello Chris.

BATH-TIME

A motor torpedo boat covered in giant bubbles silently appeared through
the early morning mists. It was only when it was almost upon us
that we could hear the muffled roar of its engines, and then only
faintly.

I have as much knowledge of myself as I do of why I was adrift in that
rubber dinghy in the Malay Straits.

All the books and maps and knowledge give us too little, leave large
blank spaces, 'terra incognita'.

". . . citizens who work and find no peace in pain.
I am chains."

In chained numbness, not confusion, the war boat bears down on me
on us where Educated Summaries are not worth a spit in hell. The
Cambridge Marxists, with large houses, cars and incomes, can
shove it.

"Anarchist Fieldmarshals, Socialist Judges, Dialectic Fuzz, Switched-
on Hangmen, and all other benefits of Correct Revolutionary
Practice."

I don't need patronage I need something else.

The mists clear before the burning sun, the sea empty and flat as a sheet
of polished metal. The long day ahead

It's the vase of tulips and a mirror trick, though this time the vase is not
    set between facing mirrors but between a mirror and a painting of
    a mirror with a vase of tulips, and this in turn photographed.

It's the beautifully printed exhibition note in front of a Korean bowl
    that has been placed on burnt umber hessian. It quotes Bernard
    Leach's praise of the "unselfconscious asymmetry" of Korean
    potters, and how nothing in nature is symmetrical, but everything
    is asymmetrical, a nose not perfectly straight, the eyes not perfectly
    level.

It's those dreams of perfection, 'the man of your dreams', 'woman of
    your dreams', 'the budgie of your dreams', 'your dreams come
    true' to a jarring chorus of cash registers and half-stifled moans.

Again and again and again and again, and the months and years glide by
    hardly noticed so heavy and dull is the obsession.

to raise your head for one moment clear of this

        skies and clouds ahead
        and the fields and cities below
        as you fly through the sunlight

And below, not looking up,
"Are you going to see the new gorillas?" he asked as we
    walked briskly towards the Jardin des Plantes.

A cold dry day in January with mist on the Downs,
    frost on the furrows and ice on the ponds.
A flock of partridges suddenly starting up in front of me,
    and whirring off to the left skimming the ploughed fields.

but André Gide wrote: "The strange mental cowardice which makes us
perpetually doubt whether future happiness can equal past happiness

is often our only cause for misery; we cling to the phantoms of our bereavements, as if we were in duty bound to prove to others the reality of our sorrow. We search after memories and wreckage, we would like to live the past over again, and we want to reiterate our joys long after they are drained to the dregs.

I hate every form of sadness, and cannot understand why trust in the beauty of the future should not prevail over worship of the past."

/Poster 2

SLEEPERS AWAKE
from the 'sensible life' whose only passion is hatred

A red and black pagoda towers above the chestnut trees
in a Royal Botanic Garden
The lush greens of south London back-gardens
O summer nights when trembling with that ecstasy
our bodies sweat and flood one another's

Burst forth—sun streams forth—light—
all doors and windows magically thrown open
a hot lush meadow outside
with dark green woods at its edges

turn it another way
These are insistences not repetitions
or the repetitions are only the insistence on

and it all crowds in:

"Nostalgia for the life of others . . . Whereas ours, seen
from the inside, seems broken up. We are still chasing
after an illusion of unity."
"Separation is the rule. The rest is chance . . ."*

which way to step?

and the dull brutality of monsters as they grind the bones
"forbidden to delight one's body, to return to the truth of things"*

The clouds part, your hand reaches through—yes
the glow and light in us, our bodies

And below around us—the flint customs house at Shoreham,
the call of a cuckoo as we climb up-hill to the Stalldown stone row,
the wild moor about, and from its edges
the churches, cathedrals, ancient and beautiful things.

Talking to myself

The sweet qualities of our dreams without which . . .

How the wind blows and our hearts ache to follow
the hazardous route the winds follow

        6 million Russians
        6 million Jews
        2 million Poles
        1 million Serbs
        Gypsies and others

*Albert Camus—*Notebooks*

O,O,O, . . . Northern California

O, rarely fingered jade sat on your blue velvet cushion
in the museum showcase.
O, handsome writing book half-bound in crimson leather
with beautifully marbled edges
sat on your exquisite and highly polished desk.
O, world of unused beauties.

Kick a stone, walk along the beach, kick the sea.
The dapper panama hat gathers dust on the cupboard's top shelf.
Dreams and more dreams. Brightly flowered vines
and the heady scent of eucalyptus trees that
with time is taken for granted and passes unnoticed.

To decorate one's life with sprays of leaves and vases of flowers.
I prepare the vase for you on the marble top of a chest of drawers.
It's just right. Will it please you? Will you notice it?
You did. Returning from your long journey
you enter the house, striding in with deeds done
and love.

That picture fades as the outside world crowds in
now. And your business continues.
My business continues.
The bright clear sunlight illuminates the headland.
A dusty pickup-truck stops outside the village store
and the dogs leap out as the driver enters.
People at the bar across the street watch this
with their usual bemused curiosity.

Someone in crisp clothing drives past on their way
out of town with their radio playing.
Through the open car window
fine phrases from an opera float out:
        "What new delights!
          What sweet sufferings!"

The dream fades. A rustling of the dry grasses
that edge the lagoon. We lost it.
And the business continues,
the daily life downtown "business as usual".

COAT OF ARMS ON WALL IN ANCIENT CITY

Bears dance to the music, slowly, awkwardly
in the grand piazza.
A thin but sufficient chain keeps them in place.

Grotesque beasts look on,
beasts cobbled together from various spare parts
and men's strange imaginations.
Is that a crocodile or an eroded dragon?
A winged lion or a sphinx?
All the world's plunder cobbled together.

Mists coat the lagoon this evening
as the ferry passes a low barge,
a pleasure launch and a small naval landing craft
on the flat waters.

In the palazzo an evening of decadence
is about to begin and the end is expectantly planned
for systematic and cold debauchery,
whips and black undergarments,
a series of calculated and delightful humiliations,
pains and pleasures.

Has the icon, looted from Cyprus, seen it all before?
The resigned virgin with child
cluttered with necklaces and improbable crowns.
A look of indifference is all we see.
She may sternly pity our fate, or
not even know it. Tough luck!
We'll get by.

We board the throbbing steamer.
Here come the bears hurrying from their last
evening performance and just in time.
"All aboard" someone shouts in Italian.
The splendours fade behind us as
we're cloaked in a sweet velvet darkness.
Ahead is the unseen landing stage,

the sound of crickets and frogs
and a bored bus driver calling to a friend.

The bears troop off and disappear into the night.
Their plans remain ambiguous.

HAND FROM AN EXETER CLOUD

Yes, now the night closes in. Yes, now the fireworks display over the cathedral has ended.
What now? The single bed in the 'guest room', the copies of Jules Laforgue's *Oeuvres complètes* at your head, distant traffic on the nearby main road?

"Is this something new?" asks the clerk
sarcastically.
Not exactly . . .

Dreams of children's voices heard the other side of a thicket. Dark green tunnels through the bushes and undergrowth. And later the next day leafing through an exhibition catalogue of Elizabethan miniatures—the sudden shock and recognition in seeing one titled "Man clasping a hand from a cloud".

SUMMER SOLSTICE

Farm boys tramp home aching from the fields.
They know where they're going, though don't
as they plod past the decaying mansion
overhung with dark trees and surrounded by damp undergrowth.
Two more miles to go and then the familiar lit rooms,
the drawers of known possessions, the familiar smells.
They will wash, eat, and go about their evening business.
But it's all far from being that simple and innocent.
Small heaps of possessions litter the landscape.
Funerals are strategically placed throughout the years.
Even rushes of vague but powerful emotions, dumb love
and feelings that cut mazes in the heart.
They pass the darkening hedges and copses
too tired from their labours to care or notice whatever,
though the next morning it could be changed possibly.
In the spacious rooms of the mansion the wind sighs
under the doors along the staircases
from the stone flagged kitchen to the cramped attics.
"Long ago and far away" a story could begin
but leaves the listeners somehow dissatisfied,
nervous on the edge of their chairs leaning forward
in contorted positions.   Waking up one day
they could set off in another direction, fresh and foreign.
They could but seldom do, so cluttered are they
and rightly distrustful of such snap solutions.
                              The farm boys proceed
to the fields, again, or turn to the factory towns.
There are glimpses caught in the dusky woods
or on a fresh summer dawn of unknown skies,
unforgettable and dazzling in their beauty. But then
the long day stretches ahead. The stirred dreams settle down
with the dust, beyond grasp or understanding.
The unseen night birds calling calling

The artful

for Anne Stevenson

A house by a lake surrounded by woods
all reflected in that lake.
Like a small round painting, like a brooch
pinned to a woman's jacket.

This picture—the miniature scene, and
the woman's soft blue tweed lapel.

Mists close in until you can see
nothing but shifting white and grey.

The air brightens and it begins to clear
into sunlight, clear you imagine
of cunning traps and the games that divert
somewhere else other than. And in the sunlight
on a bright hillside, boulders and bracken,
the mottled white crags above, the lakes below
in the distance. Not shaken free
of imagined, but been there, real as
it can be. A copper tint to the land.
Haze. Feel good, moist-eyed, opened up.
As though time suspended, almost. Red gold.

The unknown woman puts on her jacket
and strolls out of the house to the lakeside.
Autumn. No harm done.
The sun catching the polished surface
of her brooch—blue-john or brown agate.

A shepherd checks his sheep as dusk settles
in the mountains. Obscure silhouettes
that act as possible guides to get home,
to touch familiar things, never taken for granted.

Waunfawr and After/
"The collar work begins"

Ferocious gales sweep up the valley.
Heavy snow on the hills and fields.
Water flooding the roads, gushing across.
Sheets of rain slanting over the bleak
moorland, the scree slopes,
the small village post office.

I want nowhere else
but to he here,
whether crouching in a stone windbreak
on a cloud bound summit,
or coming off the slopes battered and soaked
into a dark soft tunnel of forest.
(A strange form of pleasure you may say.)

But just to be here in this place.
The deserted remote valleys
dotted with ruined farms,
hawthorn and rowan growing in their hearths.
Climbing higher to the empty cwm
with its small slashed black lake.
And on up the slopes to the bare rock ridge
and the summits again.
Nowhere else.
It's that simple, almost.

Cwm Uchaf

In Brighton someone yells from a window
        down into the dark street and . . .

On the moon in a vast barren crater
        a rock very slowly crumbles into a fine dust

A fuzz of stars sweeps across the world
        partly known and unknown dark and light

across a table top across crowded grey cells
        in a fragile bone sphere cracked and shaky

tumbling down though never that elegant or controlled
        the stumbling descent through the days' maze

Jerked back by the stars the night sky
        pinning us to the ground in glad surrender

The absurd joke painful as a rock blow
        sleep though more prolonged sweeps on and over

There is a silence you can almost touch
        its pulse lick its fingers though

never complete always a faint ringing in
        the darkness

A sighing wind the noise of distant waves
        raking a seashore

All put in a box in this cave the
        star arms remote embrace

The soft fur of an animal stepping
        out of the cave two paces four paws

Then beginning to back back

Under the stars white dots drops
        of rich red blood drip onto the floor

In unknown halls bare and functional
        as a thick orange bag on a hospital trolley

The faint glitter of the rocks mica the sky
        catching the eye stood still almost

The dust the waves going nowhere in particular
        a gradual leaking away

On the ledge

a scratched rock wall.
falling out of life
through glaring light,
no, through dark smudges,
white and grey, snow and ice,
rock.   cold air.   flashings.

a final thudding stillness.

your body stretched out in a snow patch
beside a long black boulder.

alone on the rock
in this silence.   I.   then
clawed ice of a continued ascent
weeping shouting alone on the rock.

and you gone silently   down
through grey winter air
the mountains we loved

For Paul/
Coming out of winter

On a bright winter morning
sunlight catching the tops of white buildings
a tree outlined against the sea
a wall of flints

To be able to stop and see this
the luxury   of being alive
when the waves crash on the shore
and a fresh wind streams up the narrow streets
A moment like this lightens the darkness
a little, lifts the heart until
you can walk down the hill near careless

How can that be?   suddenly slammed up
against a wall by memories of the dead
loved ones completely gone from
this place

Shafts of sunlight cutting through the clouds
onto the everchanging sea below

How many times we discussed the sea's colours
all beyond description   words a mere hint
of what's before our eyes   then and now

GILDED WHITE

for Sandy Berrigan

the snow is deep and soft on the steps
the temple roof thickly cloaked in snow
trees heavy with it
the gold carvings and red beams
luminous in the muted winter light

I look down on this from a high window
beside the window stands a tall grey feather
trimmed with charms   your gift
hung with small bells and beads and a moon
softly wrapped in wool

the day may turn   a soft dull light
to a brightness   a yellow glitter in the snow
a white cloud in a corner of the window
the ghost of a half moon in the sky

a table, a lamp, some books, a radio,
the sound of the sea in the background.
a quiet day. a cup of coffee.

on the snow covered path
or a street in a city miles away
a stillness. a middle aged woman pauses by the arch
and knocks snow from her shoes
an old man stands erect at the entrance to Via Orfeo
his cheap shirt washed ironed and neatly buttoned

Japan is a long way away   Italy is a long way away
California is a long way away   Sussex is a long way away
but all gently wrapped together in this moment
your gift

OCTOBER NIGHT

"asleep among appearances"
Octavio Paz

Strange world.
The warbling and ringing of car and shop alarms
                                             in the street,
shadows on the ceiling.
A large mauve head appearing in an ochre background.
As though a dream landscape but not.
As though a painting but not.

Eyes shut
"you were in another day"
off in the distant mountains
where the darkness breathes
and the black silhouette of a hillside
edges a charcoal grey sky.
A seeming solidity, though thin as paper.

A near astonishment at the "facts",
the surrounding sounds and sights.
The "what is this?", "who is . . . ?"
No step back possible

But a step towards?   out?

Behind your grey eyes . . .   These surfaces

A watchfulness, the distance between,
all words probing towards this puzzle.
The possible bridges?   in a clash of dreams—
though that too poetic and abstract to grasp,
shake with your hands.

A past "real", memories haunting amongst reality;
the present so . . . ?   dazed?   startled?

The colours of the dim light
projected through blinds onto a ceiling,
the feel of a cotton pillowcase on my cheek
And beyond that?

Not avoiding thought by a fence of questions,
but somehow unable . . .   to move

Clinging onto the rock face
The rain beating on the skylight
Clipped on
Floating like a sleeping angel
who then wakes touching the softness below

CHINESE THOUGHTS ON PROCEDURE

the first ice of winter
appears on the ponds, along the river banks
clear thin ice   a delicate glass
that thickens as the days follow

the first step out onto

not knowing

the small fox poised on the ice
listening listening for the telling crack

across the river the frozen willows
set in a depthless mist

Days and nights : accidental sightings
A bundle of 50 sticks for Joseph Cornell and others

a wire bent round a corner

⋆

So many pebbles on the beach, uncountable.

⋆

a silver fish reeled in from the sea. the sun glinting.

⋆

the line that says nothing. A chair creaks.

⋆

cut wood. walk the streets at night. rock'n'roll.

⋆

the wind.

⋆

fierce gusts of rain following into the night.

⋆

wind whistling and moaning around the house

⋆

stuck in the fact of absence

⋆

the air lightens—suddenly a blue sky, small white clouds
masking the sun.

⋆

the pale ochre, wheat white grass as autumn clears its way and
the rust red patches on the moor

⋆

In the town . . .

*

Making the bridges

*

. . . walking upstairs carrying a basket of wet clothes. . .

*

the wind ruffling the water of a small pond

*

the clarity of sunlight, the calm it brings, inside not outside.

*

on the cliff top

*

. . . warm from a bath . . . scented . . . simple luxuries . . .
in the night

*

a clock ticks. a silence of sorts.

*

late afternoon—coming round a corner, down a hill—the sudden
sight of a grey silk sea shining

*

towards dusk two kingfishers skimming the river
walk on and back to a town

*

that's it

*

And now..

*

(space)

*

Watching clouds through a barred window passing from the west.
White clouds   blue sky.

*

always in the present?   ing   ing

*

Where else?   or some lack of imagination?

*

a lot of anger.   a lot of death-wish.

*

"Our beards stiff with ice"—that's a memory.
(I live in a version of the past as well that can be measured
in minutes—not just the present.)

*

Other people somewhere come into this world.

*

music on the radio

*

Walk through the words.

*

the memory of a totally perfect day near indescribable—a time
of such joys and deep happiness.

*

And then out the door into a fine drizzle.

*

As Tom once wrote "this trick doesn't work."
But what trick?   A need to . . .
but what / why?   and who cares?

"Better than hanging 'round street corners," said Mother Oppen.
Really?

⋆

These words can rest here on the page, whilst dust slowly coats
the plates. A cupboard of dishes rarely used.
Grandmothers as icons.

⋆

Who needs it?

⋆

Out to sea the continually changing horizon
the qualities of light
from left to right   east to west
a startling clarity, a rain storm, more clarity shading into a
haze, a mist. Moving all the time.
And the colours?! A whole book on the colours.

⋆

sullen

⋆

Grey dark clouds, continual rain.

⋆

the alignment of stars

⋆

bare branches.

⋆

chalk white boxes.

⋆

This could go on a long time, but won't.

⋆

the word is . . . A dressing gown hung on the door.
A quietness in the house
Clock ticks   Sound of light rain falling,
dripping from the window sill.

★

clear headed

★

Distant sounds—waves breaking on the beach, traffic a street
away.

★

Bright star maps—Orion's Belt over the ploughed fields. Following
the muddy path, crossing the swollen stream, in darkness, . . .

★

a blue sky. spring coming. 8.00 a.m. on the beach, sun shining.

★

The white box contains a landscape—bare branches, a night sky
set with stars, a window, a figure, curious objects.
We look in from the outside.

AFRICAN VIOLETS

for Pansy Harwood my grandmother 1896–1989

Flags stream from the tops of the silver pyramids
Purple flowers present themselves to the air, the world
Chopin fights his way through all the notes, the choices

All this, and yet that emptiness

A real heart-breaker, tears in my eyes

What did I give you? At the last a pot of flowers,
your favourite colour, you said
then died soon after, the day after
I'd left you there in the bare hospital room
your eyes and voice so clear in the recognition
like so many years before   "O Travers"

And you gave me?   everything I know.

But to reduce this to yet another poem
to entertain

pages of words creating old routines

I systematically smash all those pretty pictures,
they won't do anymore.
"That was a bit unnecessary, son," you say.
I know, but their weight does you no service.

My blood is your blood,
it's as ancient as that;
pride and style that you had,
and with all a lovely generosity
I treasure.

I find myself moving as you would,
not the same but similar,

sharing your tastes and paths;
the night jasmin bower.

The strength of these memories
The comfort your home was

Yet it seems almost another world—
building rabbit hutches on winter evenings
in your living room, sawdust and
wood shavings on the worn carpet, easily cleared.
A house that was lived in, not exhibited.

And all those other evenings, summer or winter,
spent pickling onions, or bottling fruit,
or wrapping boxes of apples for store,
or stringing onions to hang in the shed
above the sacked potatoes,
or mending our own shoes,
all the work, cooking, making,
fixing, all done capably, easily
together.

But you now gone forever

Not sat in the corner of the couch
after your morning bath, with a cup of tea
reading the morning paper.
That ritual finished

though other "stuff" continues
as your blood continues to flow in me
no matter what I might say
(the tense continually shifts, past and present blur)
we both love(d) love and were, are natural liars,
easy with the "truth", turning facts to meet the story;
we both have a distaste for "trade"—
all the contradictions happily ignored;
we both . . .

Now wandering helpless around my room
the rich world about,
the flags and skies, the dreams

I talk to you again and again,
I see you again and again   sat there

GORGEOUS—YET ANOTHER BRIGHTON POEM

The summer's here.
Down to the beach
to swim and lounge and swim again.
Gorgeous bodies young and old.
Me too. Just gorgeous. Just feeling good
and happy and so at ease in the world.

And come early evening a red sun setting,
the sea all silky,
small gentle surges along its near still surface.

And later
the new moon hung over the sea,
a stippled band of gold across the black water,
tiger's eye.

I walk home.
The air so soft and warm,
like fur brushing my body.

The dictionary says
"**gorgeous**—adorned with rich and brilliant colours,
sumptuously splendid, showy, magnificent, dazzling."

That's right.

DREAMS OF ARMENIA

like an angel of death
telling the tale again and again
never any release

the dry rustle of feathers
behind your ear
a feather brushing your neck, your cheek

then a silence
a shadow traveller
then it starts again

★

1894 August: Sasun and surrounding villages attacked by Turks and
               Kurds. 3,000 Armenians slaughtered. "The Armenians
               were absolutely hunted like wild beasts," said H.S.
               Shipley, British representative.

1895:   Ottoman sultan puts into effect his "final solution"
               for the Armenian "problems". Special army units are
               formed. 30,000 Armenians murdered and over 8,000
               flee the country.

1896, 26-27 August: In Constantinople 6,000 murdered, the rest flee.

1896, 15-17 September: In Eghin 2,000 murdered.

1908:   "Young Turks" massacre 15,000 in Adana, and 15 to 25
               thousand in the surrounding villages. "Conservative
               estimates," say the consuls of the "Great Powers".

1915-16:   One and a half million Turkish Armenians murdered
               out of a population of three million.

The lists and details continue and continue, the facts of numberless horrors pile up endlessly like torn bodies in the Kemakh gorge.

*

In a dream a door opens
the long dead father stands there
Many others come and go
A friend enters and stays there
fixed there   the light streaming
past his silhouette   the silver edge
a bright day outside

*

If these the last words written,
words then a death, or a silence,
let them at least praise . . .
 the "Armenia" I imagine?
moonlight filling a room?
Awkward symbols,
painted boards propped
against a crumbling wall.

*

Komitas the composer silent for 20 years after watching the butchery, the massacres in a wild and empty place—neither word nor note until his death (in Paris 1935).

*

a wooden table tilted in the courtyard
an empty glass and coffee cup on one side
the heavy scent of jasmin as the evening . . .

*

Like an Armenian song that tears your heart,
like an Armenian song that tears your heart
with "memories", past loves, empty plains,
empty villages, desolate highlands, clogged ravines.

All those "things" beyond any words.

*

carved stone churches like lighthouses

And in the year 301 A.D. St. Gregory the Illuminator converted
Armenia, the first Christian kingdom in the known world.

Be praised.

And later, in 874, Princess Mariam of Siunia built a nunnery on an island
in Lake Sevan. A place to meet her fisherman lover, they say.

Be praised.

All of Armenia a massive rockbound island rising out of the surrounding
plains. A light to be praised. An illuminating beauty besieged by barbarism
and death, tides of charred destruction.

*

the silence, though not a silence,
the wind in the trees, the sound of water
somewhere, someone calling, far off,
a brief snatch of bird song nearby,
the wind in the trees, the sound of

As though a trickling—very slowly—away

*

The land still there, the sun in the sky.
The eastern provinces, Russian Armenia, still there, real enough,
crops and music and industries and dancing.
The western provinces, Turkish Armenia, there, though
the people dead or driven away. An emptiness.

*

A carved archway. An elaborately carved tomb
broken in half. Stone cut like lace.
The yellow white of grasses late in summer.

Your long black hair, an occasional grey hair,
your deep brown eyes that churn my heart.
Laughing. To touch your face,
kiss your hands and shoulders.
The poplars sway in the breeze,
their leaves twirl and sparkle silver in the sunlight.
The warmth that melts all reserves.

*

... Mkhitar Heratsi sews the wounds up with silk thread, uses mandragora
as an anaesthetic, shows for the first time (1184) how "fevers", typhoid
and malaria, are infectious, uses music for relief of nervous complaints
... A medieval beacon ... King Gayik Ardsruni of Vaspurakan builds
(915-921) a church on the island of Aghtamar in Lake Van. The outside
walls covered in relief carvings of biblical scenes. A marvel to see with
your own eyes ... The island deserted, its people long since dead, its
churches crumbling, the towers sprouting bushes and trees ...

*

Your smile, a glance caught in the market or on the river
bank. Touching as we leave a building.
The evening stroll begins in Yerevan. Lights come on in the
small outdoor cafés. Talk. The tap of backgammon pieces.
A single man's voice   singing   singing   that gives your
heart trembling wings. Then a skirl of reeds. Oboes, piccolos,
flutes, recorders, lutes, zithers and drums.
In the hot night lying together, your eyes glisten in the
soft half-light. The animal scent of our bodies.

★

fields, meadows and orchards, vineyards and pastures in a
stony land, hard and well worked and watered.
apricots, pomegranates, melons, grapes, wheat, sunflowers,
the sheep grazing.   blossom in the trees.   roses.

★

Towns, villages, churches, graveyards destroyed.
Let off the leash to murder and plunder.

But the notes, the figures, back then—1895—

8 October: Trebizond, 920 killed and 200 in the surrounding
                 villages.

21 October: Erzindjan, 260 killed and 850 in the villages.

25 October: Bitlis, 800 killed.

27 October: Baiburt, "several hundred" killed.

30 October: Erzerum, 350 killed.

1-3 November: In Diyarbekir 1,000 killed and in Arabkir 2,800.

4-9 November: Malatia, 3,000 killed.

10-11 November: Kharput, 500 killed.

28 December: Urfa, 3,000 men, women and children seeking safety in the cathedral were shot or burned to death there by Turkish troops.
"The sickening odour of roasting flesh pervaded the town" wrote Consul Fitzmaurice.

★

a silence. a door bangs in the wind.
not a dream.

★

Since the 1880s the Turkish army trained by Germans, and fully reorganised in 1913. Liman von Sanders, the German Inspector General of the Turkish Army and Freiherr Hans von Wangenheim, the German ambassador, in 1914 assist with the "master plan" for the destruction of the Armenians, a planned genocide.

"Who remembers the Armenians?" said Hitler years later as he set on the Jews.

★

Massacres, shootings, bayoneting, hacking, thrown into the Kemakh gorge, thrown into the Black Sea, deportations, forced marches, rape, starvation, robbery. Children, men, women, the old and sick.

★

They would do this to you, my love,
and to our son.

*

A summer breeze in the trees
on the hillside, on the river bank.
But the ghosts sighing,
and the crowding savages

Postscript

1   Arshile Gorky wrote in a letter, 14 February 1944, 'What has the Armenian
    experience to add to modern life? Sensitivity. That is the main, the
    unforgettable word that has been engraved in my memory of it. Sensitivity
    to beauty, sensitivity to sadness and melancholy, sensitivity to the frailty
    as well as the nobility of life. Sensitivity to mental progress. It is such an
    important contribution. Sensitivity in the day of dehumanization. There
    lies our contribution to all art. Our Armenia, the sensitivity of Armenia, its
    understanding and immense experience of bad and good, of the beautiful
    and ugly, the dead and living is needed by all the world.'

2   Beside the many books on Armenian history as a whole, the most thorough
    account of 19th and 20th century history is Christopher J. Walker's *Armenia:
    The Survival of a Nation* (Croom Helm, London, 1980).

The Songs of Those Who Are On The Sea of Glass*

A hospital room in near silence
Men in beds in varying degrees of pain
A clutter and the colour white
The bright January sun
illuminating . . .
the beige of the building opposite
The arrangement of buildings   so beautiful
Clouds and white puffs of smoke from unseen chimneys
reflected in the black windows

Waking to see this   from on high
across the morning courtyard
It's amazing

*

The bright vision fades

A battered piece is put back
on the game board
whose endlessly complicated contradictory rules
. . .. . . absurd and with no purpose

The box chipped and coated in dust
Jamaican cigars long gone
into the blue haze

*

Osip Mandelstam calls this earth
"a Godgiven palace" "the happy heaven
. . . the boundless house in which we live our lives"

*

The living dead plod across the ice to
stare through thick glass walls
"Let me in!"   "Let me out!"

114

As though floating. Couldn't care less.
Which side.   Outside.   Down there.

The ice window
(that's a metaphor)
Climbing over the bones
(that's a metaphor)
Aquarium walls

Grotesque gawping fish
Nightmare stuff

A new moon high in the sky over the sea

*

Suddenly keeling over
A blur
Dream ambulances, rooms, people, tubes

Back and forth over the river

But love and duty call and pull,
Stoic virtues make it amusing,
the whimpers and begging—a story.

*

Talking in code ?

*

A rawness.   The rediscovered face in the mirror
"I know you?"   Mid-morning.
Washed and shaved
A body stitched and wired together. The Creature.

"The monster! The monster!" fleeing villagers yell
in black and white Transylvania.

"I don't need, I don't need . . ."

Emptiness would soothe
A bare room   no clutter

*

The sea was frozen as we approached Esbjerg
the crunch and crack of ice beneath the ferry's bow
as it ploughed on towards a grey line in the whiteness

Inland a fox trotted nervously
across snow-covered fields and streams

The warmth of the cabin bunk, of the den,
of the sun when it breaks through
and, wrapped up, you skim stones across
a small frozen pool in the mountains,
the ricochet ringing, whining,
a high singing.

*

black glass windows
across the courtyard
reflections of clouds, columns of smoke
Bright January sun
a glitter in the air
that fills rooms
(a gold-leaf annunciation)

As though reborn
not racked with loss, past if-onlys
To walk at ease with the ghosts
(not a club member yet)
warm and open and thankful

with care
it seems possible

sat up in bed in bizarre pyjamas

[* title of the volume of Welsh hymns by William Williams (Pantycelyn), published c1750: 'Caniadau y Rhai sydd ar y Mor a Wydr'.]

PAGHAM HARBOUR SPRING

The blur of sky and sea
this white grey morning
before the day burns
moves into blue

the sweet butter scent of gorse
the sweet scent of you
dear daughter   ghost in my head
dear daughter

the mudflats and saltings shine
as the children run by
along marsh edge and the high dyke bank
egret and oystercatcher   dunlin and sandpiper

In the distance a train passes
where a short neat man
pushes a refreshment trolley
his clean white shirt immaculately ironed
his black waistcoat just right
the quiet dignity of him
as he passes through the hours

You'd know this   the particulars
were you here
held in the wide sky arc
the children running on the dyke bank
absorbed in this world

Salt Water*

The complexity of a coral reef
the creatures   sunlight
shafting down through crystal sea
water   the flicker of shadows
light wavering and fading
into the depths

Near the silver mirrored surface
bright yellow fish
flutter through the reef
crowded with the swaying tendrils
of coral and anemones,
smudges of algae, drifts of seaweed,
starfish and shellfish flowing
through the canyons

The sun rises three times
The sun sets three times

over sea   over land

on land
her blue grey eyes gaze at the world
in silence   blink at the world
the world goes about
its usual business

"A fine view along the coast"
to be seen from a high building's
window   one of many windows

"Polyps" the books say   coral
a tube with a mouth at the end
surrounded by tendrils to catch
small creatures
A world of soft tissue
And the colours
white   red   orange

yellow   green   blue
purple   "natural pigments"
and those too changeable
when algae "lives within the tissue"

Many species   Many depths
and the light filtered down
reducing reducing

And bright yellow fish
banded with peacock blue
flutter through the reef
Red fish   Black fish
with lemon ringed eyes
flutter through the reef

How delighted she'd be
Her blue grey eyes gazing at this world
while cradled in her mother's
her father's arms
the world going about its usual business

A ship's bows cut the salt water
a phosphorescent trail in the tropic night

The phosphorus glitter of the sea
From the Greek
phos (light)—phoros (bringing)

Like her
as she came and went

Morning star

* In memory of Joey Peirce / Harwood, who lived 11–14 March 1997.

THE WIND RISES : ISTVAN MARTHA MEETS SANDY BERRIGAN

After the goodbyes
the first steps out
across the ice and snow.

As though the first steps
of one's life. white breath.
one foot after another.

A black wind-torn night
and the sound of footsteps
crunching on unseen ice.

A glaring light trembles
on the side of a distant cowshed.
We get older.

The past autumn a memory
that now warms us.
A journey back to the city.

An old woman and her grandchild
climbing into the provincial train
carrying baskets of dark plums.

Dogs barked at the edge of a village
as crumbling cement walls faded
into a soft smoky dusk.

The last clamour of rooks,
a distant car barely seen not heard,
the clatter of a helicopter flying low home.

From that dusk into this night
so quick despite the weeks.
Shocked back into the present.

In your cabin you lean forward
to sew a quilt or read a letter.
Leagues away I enter this darkness.

In the black cold I . . .   you . . .
A curtain is pulled closed.
To reach sleep one way or another.

But wherever, the ghosts are with us.
We live with them, that loss.
Loved ones gone one way or another.

Dead or alive they are with us
sharing a view, a joke, some music.
Guiding or grieving us.

Is that what getting old is?
Learning to live like this—that strength
increasingly needed. Or sink into gaga?

And by day the thud of machines,
the high whine of the saw mill,
the clicking of keyboards and tills.

The swish of a broom as a man
sweeps the gutter, the swish of your broom
as you sweep the homes of the wealthy.

Winter birds clear against a grey sky.
As night falls snow falls
on near silent factories, heavy forests.

You lean towards the light, pause.
"Neighbour-calls in the dark".
Tender-hipped you dream, dear heart.

Not forever in this chilling night,
I know, there are places to go.
Stumbling over frozen ruts and furrows.

One foot after another
steering through half-known outlines,
the black silhouettes of hills and trees.

The ghosts are quiet,
minding their own business,
warming their hands in Kapolcs or Capel.

Pole star "to a foreign land"
where no one will follow
in black or white or "golden gown".

ERIK SATIE

As simple as that

a piano in a cluttered room
high above the suburbs
factory chimneys railway bridges

to make a heart melt and lurch

On the train back to the centre
a crazy woman repeating repeating
"un voleur des anges   un voleur des anges"
angel thief   angel thief
again and again

To calm her . . .   Nothing
can touch her

Cwm Nantcol

for Anne Stevenson and Peter Lucas

1

Light slanting down on this high green valley.
Wind blowing, bending the reeds, hawthorn trees,
the scattered clumps of rowans.

Massive slabs of rock,
like ribs down the sides of the cwm,
clawed and scoured, ground and polished
by the glaciers of "Ancient Times".
And now silver birch, oaks, tender mosses
grow in the shadows of these purple grey bluffs.

Such an emptiness. Here where sheep die
trapped in a fence or drowned in the river,
where a single track winds up into the mountains,
ends at the last farm, a stream, cattle
up to their shanks in a bog, a leaning
telephone pole among giant scattered boulders.

A near silence broken by the sound of
a raven's wing-beat as it flies
high above, fast across a clear blue sky;
the sound of waterfalls in the distance.

That's it, all that's present, or so it feels.

But why this fascination? the many returns
to this place? A comfort? Seeming timeless moments
when stood here in the sweep of the mountains.

2

The Polish general in that shrinking army camp, near late 1940's Nantwich, planted out his garden. Wherever he was, planted out the same garden—his only gravity among all the moves and changes. The neat rows of raddish, onions, cabbage, carrots, and dill to go on the potatoes. And lots of flowers—marigolds, sweet williams, sweet peas. A home. And a deep pit to store potatoes for the winter. A clamp. A deep safe cellar.

3

And back here in the west a high sprung hare
gallops away, disturbed on the hillside.

Later, the winter sun warm on my face,
I sit on a rock surrounded by bog myrtle,
the colours of the mountains, the patches of
blond gold grasses and red copper bracken.
A stillness beyond words.

Not denying the distant city.

The darkness of late afternoon is near
and sudden. A pale line of sea on the horizon.

from FIVE PIECES FOR FIVE PHOTOS

for Lou Esterman wherever he may be.

1. The Surveyor's Office at the Custom House, Salem, where Nathaniel Hawthorne worked 1846-1849.

It's a dream, an escape of sorts that does work in its fashion—the solitary life, "peace", and no demands. A neat life, marred by an ageing fussiness, the fading of friendships, times of undeniable loneliness. And yet those days when bright sunlight holds the room and there is an indescribable quiet.

I know what is in every drawer, on each shelf. Inscribe in the ledger these details?   Hesitant.   No, let it be.

Outside the door the sound of people running down the stairs

5. Mother and Child in a Restaurant Garden.

> We smile at the children
> absorbed and open in their world,
> with warm hearts
> watch them and their young parents.
>
> We're older, our bodies too—
> your silken sagging breasts,
> my scrawny arms.
> Yet when we laugh together,
> are happy in each other's company,
> touch, embrace, feel that love,
> then . . .   All the tussles fade.
> Moments of anger and estrangement
> between couples, within families,
> resentments, lies, and unfading scars,
> disappear like rocks in the mist.

Blown pink roses hang on their stems
in the garden or hedgerow.
Their scent not powerful nor obvious
until you put your face in their petals.

There are dusty plateaux around Rudina in Hercegovina. Only the hardiest grasses can grow in their near barren soil, fit only for flocks of goats and sheep. Of the few that live there most families leave in the winter, unable to bear its hardships. It's the embodiment of the vukojebinje of south Slavic lore. This Serbo-Croat word translates as "the land where wolves fuck".

To come from there and make something
—is that a question or an exhortation?

Hampton Court shelter

That hue of light you find on a summer afternoon
when a rain storm batters the gardens, stitches the heavy river.
Like dusk but not.

You and I in a room set with windows overlooking that river.
A room panelled with large mirrors, long smoky mirrors
whose foxed glass reflects our dusky selves, maybe our ghosts.
And inbetween—the window seats and views of a flowing watery world.

That this 17th century pavilion, built for privacy and banquets,
could have been where voyages were planned, trade calculated
and profit, much profit, inbetween the laughter.

That the elaborate maze-like gardens that surround this pavilion
are where people wandered talking,
are where we will soon wander in a fine rain
unaware of anything beyond, caught in the moment's delight

as we weave our way through the flower beds, the sunken gardens,
the arched corridors of wisteria, pergolas of laburnum,
honey scented lime walks, our myths and histories laid aside.
Floating in any century, timeless, we romantically imagine.

If the myths were put aside, and we . . . ?
Would the mirrors be clear and glitter?   a rainbow
flickering on their bevelled edges?   I doubt it.

"So what are you going to do
with the rest of your life?"

from GIFTS RECEIVED : SIX POEMS FOR FRIENDS

1
'From the highest window of her chronology'*
she saw the beanstalk, she let her blond gold hair
flow down the tower to be met by
no prince, no dragon, no statesman.
The chronology of her anger
The chronology of her disappointments
                                        printed on her body.
"I have eaten the laurel leaves
and cannot tell what I say."

Chronos in the nearby woodpile
watches, amused. He's in no hurry.
That's all relative. The height of a window?
Years pass and the brambles grow.
Whatever she says—the messages will
tumble into a blankness, mulch down
into incomprehensible phrases.
And the sun will shine, beans grow,
a faded fox trot through the clearing.

3
There is no second chance. *
The baggage left at the station stays there,
the steel lockers' dull glitter in the shadows.

A full moon and low tide.
Easter or whatever spring festival
you choose   To start fresh . . .

A morning when—on a sun bright beach
dried seaweed, shells amongst the shingle
—all seems present, not scattered.

But so many years pass
darkened by regrets and funerals.
If that could be put aside?

And then waiting for the next step
surrounded by strangers in our new world?
That isn't real. No complaints.

Fumble, stumble on. And what is
in the luggage, anyway?
the usual selfish cruelties, the usual warmths?

"You're not **that** special," said
the railway employee under his breath.

"Marvellous," said a rangey man
wandering the beach picking up twigs.

But a nagging emptiness—a life without love.
Untouched with no one to hold. That simple.

A life pulled back by heavy dreams
not pushed forward with tender hopes.

The sea so calm and the water clear.
When swimming you can see ever detail of the seabed.

The bags and cases are stacked neatly
ready for eventual removal by the authorities.

5
where language falters   near struck dumb
to try to say   what matters
and what's so far from clear   so beyond the words

the outlines blur   of that dark shadow
that heavily cloaks days and nights

a line of rooftops against the night sky
rain and mist blowing through a clump of trees

[Enter the Gloom Monster
He thinks he's set up]

Past the middle of my life
sleepless, in no dark wood
the usual streets out there

Spurred by neither love nor loss of love
just the usual facts of time draining away
the body's ageing, pointless regret, and loneliness

Then an unexpected gift arrives—a Mexican bus ticket

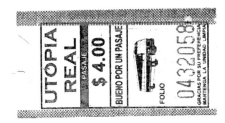

The brightly coloured bus
—trinkets jingling, saints swaying,
all the music the driver could want—
drives into and out of my dream

The dream of "utopia real" stays
day and night

To step from dream back into daily life . . . ?
maybe clear eyed and fresh in this world

The woodlouse uncurls and trots out from behind the skirting-board

"Two tickets, please, for the Gloom Monster and me."
        or to be in character
"Dos pasajes, por favor. Uno para mi y el otro para el Señor Agonías."

6
A city laid out with its web of streets shown as
an 18th century engraving drawn by an impossible bird.
And the vast square.

In the square the old market hall, and that surrounded by
restaurants, cafes, bars, banks, and a tall brick church.
A passageway leads off into a courtyard.

Three people stand in the courtyard staring at an ancient clock
                            set above them among all the windows.
Windows to many rooms, large and small, bright and dark.
In one room . . .

Standing beside a table. In the winter light.
"It's all about ambivalence," he said. And rightly so.
Though such a coldness counters dreams of celebrations.

The three turn and leave the courtyard
to continue their tour of the 'old quarter'
and maybe visit the market in plac Nowy.

"Where were you going?" A glass of black tea on the table.
"I'm not sure," I replied. A government clerk in his office imagined.
In the book—"the delight and grief of time"

Shoo that stuff into the box for a while.
Snow flakes frozen to the windowpanes.
No need to look at your watch.

Later taking the tram out to the edge of town.
The blocks of workers' flats near the extinct steel mills.
Broken lifts, graffitied stairwells.

At the door to the flat—fifth floor—
"No, Piotr isn't here. We don't know when he'll be back,
but come in, wait if you like."

The flat crowded with family, children running around,
a large dog banging the furniture with its tail.
A plate of makaroniki is placed on the table.

As the afternoon passes I'm left by the window watching
plastic bags stuck in the bare trees below,
grubby flags for whatever.

Maybe settle down with the family talking
"And how is Miron?"—Where are you Piotr?—
or make my way back into town.

At dusk freezing fog begins to fill the square.
In the bright arcade the price of amber is higher than the visitors expected.
What do you want?   an ABC?

The warmth of an amber necklace around your neck.

Did the emperor's poem mention this?

Notes
1.*A line dictated to Anne Stevenson in a dream. My thanks to her for letting
   me steal it.
3.*This line is taken from Ian Davidson's poem "No way back". My thanks for
   its loan.
5. The Mexican bus ticket was sent to me by Wanda Zyborska and is now
   greatly treasured.
6. For Piotr Sommer and Lindy, and with gratitude to Xu Yang for painting
   "Bird's Eye View of the Capital" for the Qianlong Emperor's 1767 poem.

FRAMES

for John Hall

Walk through the mirror into that other world.
A darkness at first—as though in a dream—
or dazed waking in the middle of the night—
then to find yourself at the river's mouth,
pulled, carried, back and forth by the tide
or the river, depending on moon or rain.

You rarely leave the water and are surprised
on doing so—the surrounding marshes,
a wide landscape of levels and hills,
with attendant birds. The blackness of the mirror
catches flashes, fragments of light. You pass
back and forth. Mercury sliding off your skin.

Are your days on the frontier over? Banished
for your ignorance. And still blind
to what passes maybe even now? The
days and nights where no lessons are learned
or were learned. Useless words and as though in slow motion
sleep walking, raising a hand, tilting your head.

In the orchid pavilion your imagined other self
steps back through the mirror that isn't even there.
A heron flies slowly up and down that river.
The frontier could lie across a desert or scrubland
or a mountain ridge or an ordinary backyard.
Do you remember the moth orchids dancing?

Dancing, trembling in a breeze or as someone brushed
past their declining colours. A workman passes carrying
a sheet of glass—repairs are needed. The exile,
the ignorance continues. And how is it pushed beyond
its obscure borders? I mean the ignorance.
What's beyond that sandy slope, over that bright green hill?

An idyllic life in a fuggy yurt? Dawns of amazing clarity?
It's alright for those engineers precisely marking out the
path of a wall, for those silk robed philosophers poised
in the yellow pavilion. Over here in the dust, the mud,
or—on better days—simply swept in circles by the river,
relaxed and staring up at the sky, the ambition is hard to define.

"Cloudy Sunday"

The flat plain
covered in a thin layer of snow,
with clumps of trees
here and there, dark and bare.
Snow and mud. The deep cold.

Muddy ruts, tracks, head off
disappearing into the December mist.
And through the middle of this world
a straight road, its dull glitter,
precisely straight.

Off in the distance the small village—
a crowd by the roadside waiting
to climb into a bus,
a market with little or nothing
to sell or buy. Standing around.

The memory of
those rows of long wooden huts fades,

fades, numbed by alcohol
and tiredness from work.
But some nights, lying in bed,
clear headed,
it's there
again

and that knowledge.

There are things we can barely write about.
This is not a matter of secrets
but things so terrible . . .
But no excuse in ignorance
nor—maybe—silence.

The perversion of calculated cruelty
unknown to other animals.
Such frail creatures
capable of such cowardly brutality.
I cannot describe, but I know, have seen.

"if you're an electrician you'll live"

Mourning the dead never ends.
Sideboard, couch, spoon, hair brush.
You've read the books, seen the photos.
You know what I mean.
"if you're an electrician . . . "

And back at the market
a man stands holding out a single black jacket,
an old woman lays out worn stockings on a table,
a young woman holds a tray with
8 boxes of matches.

To the south, in the late afternoon,
people assemble in a town square,
flecks of snow in the air
later shifting to a fine drizzle.
The repetitions   ahead

remembering forgetting remembering   again and again

COMPARATIVE ANATOMY :
A HOMAGE TO MICHEL-EUGÈNE CHEVREUL (1786–1889)

A herd of skeletons
charges towards you as
you enter this 19th century hall
of dark wood, high ceilings and galleries.
Tapirs, foxes, wolves, deer, horses,
not forgetting man and his monkey chums,
and bringing up the rear two elephants,
two giraffes, several walruses and three whales.

Where is Monsieur Chevreul?
He will soothe them, stop them in their tracks,
halt the stampede.

He is out on his pedestal,
snow on his head, shoulders, and hunched back,
the sleeves of his coat and shoes.
All around him the deserted gardens of
the Muséum National d'Histoire Naturelle.

He's not lost his way nor is lost in thought.
His attention is as focused as ever.
That kindly smile (we so long for)
that brings calm and a clear knowledge
that somehow all will be explained or nearly so.

It's wrong that I long for the hours to pass,
long for the time of sleep.
Riddle my head with thoughts of an empty desk
—who will use it again?—or a worn chair
thrown in a skip.
That I long for my father long gone,
for the words never said, the quiet company
rarely known. The questions whose answers
will never come. Impossible maundering.

Here's Monsieur Chevreul. He'll soothe them,
soothe me. He'll take us to the hot houses.
He will stand in awe with an Indian father
and his daughters and me before a mauve veined orchid
or a dusty pink orchid with chestnut brown spots.
He'll explain Darwin's findings on their propagation.
He'll explain his own theory of colours to us.

This may seem to have wandered.
The skeletons are getting restless,
still want to exit, explore, or
just gallop around the gardens.
To run off into the distance
—though where then? to start a new life?
and how would it really work?
The clatter of hooves on some empty concourse?

How white the bones are, and how amazing their forms.
Who would have thought a giraffe's neck bones were so long?

Monsieur Chevreul has gone off for now.
Being over a hundred he's decided to study
the effects of ageing on the human body.

"Harmony and contrast" he wrote,
in translation, of colour.

Printed in the United Kingdom
by Lightning Source UK Ltd.
133911UK00002B/310-330/P